FISCAL YEAR 2019

EFFICIENT, EFFECTIVE, ACCOUNTABLE

AN
AMERICAN BUDGET

MAJOR SAVINGS AND REFORMS

BUDGET OF THE U.S. GOVERNMENT

OFFICE OF MANAGEMENT AND BUDGET | OMB.GOV

GENERAL NOTES

1. All years referenced for budget data are fiscal years unless otherwise noted. All years referenced for economic data are calendar years unless otherwise noted.

2. At the time of this writing, none of the full-year appropriations bills for 2018 have been enacted, therefore, the programs and activities normally provided for in the full-year appropriations bills were operating under a continuing resolution (Public Law 115-56, division D, as amended). In addition, the Additional Supplemental Appropriations for Disaster Relief Requirements Act, 2017 (Public Law 115-72, division A) provided additional appropriations for 2018 for certain accounts within the Departments of Agriculture, Homeland Security, and the Interior. The Department of Defense Missile Defeat and Defense Enhancements Appropriations Act, 2018 (Public Law 115-96, division B) also provided additional appropriations for 2018 for certain accounts within the Department of Defense. Accordingly, references to 2018 spending in the text and tables reflect the levels provided by the continuing resolution and, if applicable, Public Laws 115-72 (division A) and 115-96 (division B).

3. The Budget does not incorporate the effects of Public Law 115-120, including the reauthorization of the Children's Health Insurance Program and amendments to the tax code in that law.

4. Detail in this document may not add to the totals due to rounding.

U.S. GOVERNMENT PUBLISHING OFFICE, WASHINGTON 2018

Table of Contents

Department of Energy

Department of Health and Human Services

Department of Homeland Security

Department of Housing and Urban Development

Department of the Interior

Department of Justice

Department of Labor

Department of State and U.S. Agency for International Development

Department of Transportation

Department of the Treasury

Environmental Protection Agency

National Aeronautics and Space Administration

Other Independent Agencies

Mandatory Reforms

Multi-Agency

Department of Agriculture

Department of Commerce

Department of Education

Department of Energy

Department of Health and Human Services

Corps of Engineers

Office of Personnel Management

Other Independent Agencies

MAJOR SAVINGS AND REFORMS IN THE PRESIDENT'S 2019 BUDGET

This volume describes major savings and reform proposals included in the 2019 President's Budget. It includes both discretionary and mandatory savings proposals that work to bring Federal spending under control, and reduce deficits by $3.6 trillion over the budget window. These proposals encompass an aggressive set of actions to redefine the proper role of the Federal Government and curtail those programs that fail to efficiently and effectively deliver promised outcomes to the American people.

In total, this volume highlights 2019 proposed savings of $48.4 billion in discretionary programs, including $25.8 billion in program eliminations and $22.6 billion in reductions. The volume also describes the major mandatory savings proposals summarized in Table S-6 of the *Budget* volume. Many of the eliminations and reductions in this volume reflect a continuation of policies proposed in the 2018 President's Budget that have not yet been enacted by the Congress. New savings and reforms proposals focus on the Administration's efforts to eliminate waste, fraud, and abuse in Federal programs. Notable new proposals would strengthen the ability for programs such as Medicare and Medicaid to detect and prevent fraud, protecting beneficiaries from harm and improving payment accuracy and reporting; where other proposals reflect the Administration's efforts to shift critical resources to the most pressing and highest-priority areas, such as national defense and homeland security.

The Administration will continue to build on these proposals in order to implement the President's charge to reform the Federal Government and reduce the Federal civilian workforce. The savings and reform proposals included in this volume continue, and expand on, the Administration's efforts to create an efficient, effective and accountable Government.

MAJOR DISCRETIONARY ELIMINATIONS
(Budget Authority in Millions)

	2017 Enacted	2019 Request	2019 Change from 2017
Agriculture			
Forest Service Land Acquisition	56	....	−56
McGovern-Dole International Food for Education	202	....	−202
Rural Business and Cooperative Service	103	....	−103
Rural Water and Wastewater Grants	509	....	−509
Single Family Housing Direct Loans	68	....	−68
Total, Agriculture	**938**	**........**	**−938**
Commerce			
Economic Development Administration	266	15	−251
Manufacturing Extension Partnership	130	5	−125
National Oceanic and Atmospheric Administration Grants and Education	273	....	−273
Total, Commerce	**669**	**20**	**−649**
Education			
21st Century Community Learning Centers	1,192	....	−1,192
Comprehensive Literacy Development Grants	190	....	−190
Federal Supplemental Educational Opportunity Grants	733	....	−733
Gaining Early Awareness and Readiness for Undergraduate Programs (GEAR UP)	340	....	−340
Impact Aid Payments for Federal Property	69	....	−69
International Education	72	....	−72
Promise Neighborhoods	73	....	−73
Statewide Longitudinal Data Systems	32	....	−32
Strengthening Institutions	87	....	−87
Student Support and Academic Enrichment Grants	400	....	−400
Supporting Effective Instruction State Grants	2,044	....	−2,044
Teacher Grant Programs			
School Leader Recruitment and Support	15	....	−15
Supporting Effective Educative Development (SEED)	65	....	−65
Teacher and School Leader Incentive Grants	200	....	−200
Teacher Quality Partnership	43	....	−43
Technical Assistance Programs			
Comprehensive Centers	50	....	−50
Regional Education Labs	54	....	−54
Total, Education	**5,659**	**........**	**−5,659**
Energy			
Advanced Research Projects Agency - Energy	305	....	−305
Department of Energy Loan and Loan Guarantee Programs	17	−1	−18
Mixed Oxide Fuel Fabrication Facility Termination	335	279	−56
Total, Energy	**657**	**278**	**−379**
Health and Human Services			
Agency for Healthcare Research and Quality [1]	324	....	−324
Community Services Block Grant	715	....	−715
Health Workforce Programs	539	88	−451
Low Income Home Energy Assistance Program	3,390	....	−3,390
Total, Health and Human Services	**4,968**	**88**	**−4,880**
Homeland Security			
Transportation Security Administration Law Enforcement Grants	45	....	−45
Total, Homeland Security	**45**	**........**	**−45**
Housing and Urban Development			
Choice Neighborhoods	138	−138	−276
Community Development Block Grant	3,000	....	−3,000
HOME Investment Partnerships Program	950	....	−950
Self-Help and Assisted Homeownership Opportunity Program Account	54	....	−54
Total, Housing and Urban Development	**4,142**	**−138**	**−4,280**
Interior			
Abandoned Mine Land Grants	105	....	−105
Centennial Challenge Fund	20	....	−20

MAJOR DISCRETIONARY ELIMINATIONS—Continued
(Budget Authority in Millions)

	2017 Enacted	2019 Request	2019 Change from 2017
Heritage Partnership Program	20	....	−20
National Wildlife Refuge Fund	13	....	−13
Total, Interior	**158**	....	**−158**
Justice			
State Criminal Alien Assistance Program	210	....	−210
Total, Justice	**210**	....	**−210**
Labor			
Indian and Native American Program	50	....	−50
Migrant and Seasonal Farmworker Training	82	....	−82
OSHA Training Grants	11	....	−11
Senior Community Service Employment Program	400	....	−400
Total, Labor	**543**	....	**−543**
State and USAID			
Development Assistance	2,835	....	−2,835
Earmarked Appropriations for Non-Profit Organizations			
The Asia Foundation	17	....	−17
East-West Center	17	....	−17
Global Climate Change Initiative	160	....	−160
P.L. 480 Title II Food Aid	1,600	....	−1,600
Total, State and USAID	**4,629**	....	**−4,629**
Transportation			
National Infrastructure Investments (TIGER)	500	....	−500
Total, Transportation	**500**	....	**−500**
Treasury			
Multilateral Agricultural Development Programs			
Global Agriculture and Food Security Program	23	....	−23
International Fund for Agricultural Development	30	....	−30
Total, Treasury	**53**	....	**−53**
National Aeronautics and Space Administration			
Five Earth Science Missions	133	....	−133
Office of Education	100	....	−100
WFIRST Space Telescope	105	....	−105
Total, National Aeronautics and Space Administration	**338**	....	**−338**
Other Independent Agencies			
Chemical Safety Board	11	9	−2
Corporation for National and Community Service	1,030	123	−907
Corporation for Public Broadcasting	495	15	−480
D.C. Tuition Assistance Grants	40	....	−40
Institute of Museum and Library Services	231	23	−208
International Development Foundations			
African Development Foundation	30	5	−25
Inter-American Foundation	22	3	−19
Legal Services Corporation	385	18	−367
National Endowment for the Arts	150	29	−121
National Endowment for the Humanities	150	42	−108
Neighborhood Reinvestment Corporation	140	27	−113
Regional Commissions			
Delta Regional Authority	25	3	−22
Denali Commission	17	7	−10
Northern Border Regional Commission	10	1	−9
U.S. Trade and Development Agency	75	12	−63
Woodrow Wilson International Center for Scholars	11	7	−4
Total, Other Independent Agencies	**2,822**	**324**	**−2,498**
Total Major Discretionary Eliminations	**26,331**	**572**	**−25,759**

[1] 2019 NIH Request includes $256 million to consolidate AHRQ activities.

MAJOR DISCRETIONARY REDUCTIONS
(Budget Authority in Millions)

	2017 Enacted	2019 Request	2019 Change from 2017
Agriculture			
Agricultural Quarantine Inspection User Fee	29	....	−29
Animal and Plant Health Inspection Service	952	739	−213
Conservation Operations	864	669	−195
Economic Research Service	77	45	−32
Federal Grain Inspection Service User Fee	20	....	−20
Total, Agriculture	**1,942**	**1,453**	**−489**
Education			
Federal Work Study	990	200	−790
Total, Education	**990**	**200**	**−790**
Energy			
Applied Energy Programs	3,776	1,696	−2,080
Total, Energy	**3,776**	**1,696**	**−2,080**
Health and Human Services			
National Institute for Occupational Safety and Health	335	200	−135
Office of the National Coordinator for Health Information Technology	60	38	−22
Total, Health and Human Services	**395**	**238**	**−157**
Homeland Security			
Flood Hazard Mapping and Risk Analysis Program	178	100	−78
Total, Homeland Security	**178**	**100**	**−78**
Housing and Urban Development			
Grants to Native American Tribes and Alaska Native Villages	714	600	−114
Rental Assistance Programs	38,098	33,816	−4,282
Total, Housing and Urban Development	**38,812**	**34,416**	**−4,396**
Interior			
Federal Land Acquisition	154	8	−146
Total, Interior	**154**	**8**	**−146**
Justice			
COPS Hiring Program	195	99	−96
Total, Justice	**195**	**99**	**−96**
Labor			
Bureau of International Labor Affairs	86	19	−67
Job Corps	1,704	1,297	−407
Office of Disability Employment Policy	38	27	−11
Total, Labor	**1,828**	**1,343**	**−485**
State and USAID			
Educational and Cultural Exchanges	634	159	−475
International Organization Contributions (Base Budget Authority)	1,602	899	−703
Overseas Contingency Operations	20,785	12,017	−8,768
Peacekeeping (Base Budget Authority)	688	356	−332
Total, State and USAID	**23,709**	**13,431**	**−10,278**
Transportation			
Capital Investment Grants (New Starts)	2,413	1,000	−1,413
Essential Air Service	150	93	−57
Grants to Amtrak	1,495	738	−757
Railroad Safety User Fee	....	−50	−50
Total, Transportation	**4,058**	**1,781**	**−2,277**
Treasury			
Community Development Financial Institutions Fund	248	14	−234
Special Inspector General for the Troubled Asset Relief Program	41	18	−23
Total, Treasury	**289**	**32**	**−257**

MAJOR DISCRETIONARY REDUCTIONS—Continued

(Budget Authority in Millions)

	2017 Enacted	2019 Request	2019 Change from 2017
Environmental Protection Agency			
Categorical Grants	1,066	597	−469
Energy Star and Voluntary Climate Programs	66	....	−66
Research and Development	475	246	−229
Superfund	1,089	762	−327
Total, Environmental Protection Agency	**2,696**	**1,605**	**−1,091**
Other Independent Agencies			
U.S Institute of Peace	38	20	−18
Total, Other Independent Agencies	**38**	**20**	**−18**
Total Major Discretionary Reductions	**79,060**	**56,422**	**−22,638**

MANDATORY SAVINGS PROPOSALS
(Outlays and Receipts in Millions of Dollars)

	Five-Year Savings 2019-2023	Ten-Year Savings 2019-2028
Multi-Agency		
Conduct Spectrum Auctions Below 6 Gigahertz	−600	−6,600
Eliminate Allocations to the Housing Trust Fund and Capital Magnet Fund	−1,301	−3,363
Reduce Improper Payments and Other Program Integrity [1]	−19,673	−187,640
Reform Federal Disability Programs [1]	−9,001	−72,012
Reform Medical Liability	−10,557	−52,119
Repeal and Replace Obamacare	−98,233	−674,706
Agriculture		
Eliminate Food for Progress Food Aid Program	−830	−1,660
Eliminate Interest Payments to Electric and Telecommunications Utilities	−644	−1,289
Eliminate the Rural Economic Development Program	−318	−318
Establish Agricultural Marketing Service User Fee	−100	−200
Establish Animal and Plant Health Inspection Service User Fee	−115	−230
Establish Food Safety and Inspection Service User Fee	−2,640	−5,940
Establish Packers and Stockyards Program User Fee	−115	−230
Farm Bill Savings	−17,466	−47,039
Reform the Supplemental Nutrition Assistance Program	−98,224	−213,526
Commerce		
Lease Shared Secondary Licenses	−285	−670
Education		
Create Single Income-Driven Repayment Plan	−43,568	−128,365
Eliminate Account Maintenance Fee Payments to Guaranty Agencies	−656	−656
Eliminate Public Service Loan Forgiveness	−17,834	−45,862
Eliminate Subsidized Student Loans	−12,931	−28,555
Energy		
Divest the Power Marketing Administrations' Transmission Assets	−3,792	−5,788
Reform the Laws Governing How the Power Marketing Administrations Establish Power Rates	−874	−1,899
Repeal Borrowing Authority for Western Area Power Administration	−550	−640
Health and Human Services		
Eliminate the Social Services Block Grant	−8,160	−16,660
Medicaid: Address Wasteful Spending, Fraud, and Abuse	....	−19,470
Medicaid: Drug Pricing and Payment Improvements	−170	−404
Medicaid: Strengthen Operations and Increase State Flexibility	−2,260	−5,580
Medicare and Medicaid: Increase Oversight of Opioid Prescriptions and Expand Treatment Options	−195	−965
Medicare: Address Fraud and Abuse [1]	−361	−915
Medicare: Drug Pricing and Payment Improvements	−2,475	−5,316
Medicare: Eliminate Wasteful Federal Spending	−78,294	−266,191
Reduce the Grace Period for Exchange Premiums	−1,300	−1,300
Strengthen the Child Support Enforcement Program	−265	−1,384
Temporary Assistance for Needy Families Reforms	−10,217	−21,257
Homeland Security		
Establish an Immigration Services Surcharge	−2,397	−5,166
Extend Expiring Customs and Border Protection Fees	....	−12,758
Increase Customs User Fees	−686	−1,696
Increase Worksite Enforcement Penalties	−72	−147
Reauthorize Oil Spill Liability Trust Fund Excise Tax	−2,262	−4,785
Interior		
Cancel Southern Nevada Public Lands Management Act Balances	−230	−230
Reauthorize the Federal Land Transaction Facilitation Act	−35	−35
Repeal Enhanced Geothermal Payments to Counties	−20	−40

MANDATORY SAVINGS PROPOSALS—Continued
(Outlays and Receipts in Millions of Dollars)

	Five-Year Savings 2019-2023	Ten-Year Savings 2019-2028
Labor		
Establish an Unemployment Insurance Solvency Standard	−4,478	−11,111
Improve Pension Benefit Guaranty Corporation Solvency	−6,383	−15,730
Reform the Federal Employees' Compensation Act (FECA)	−84	−117
Reform the Trade Adjustment Assistance Program	−1,168	−1,744
Treasury		
Debt Collections Proposals		
Increase Delinquent Federal Non-tax Debt Collections	−160	−320
Increase and Streamline Recovery of Unclaimed Assets	−40	−80
Increase and Extend Guarantee Fee Charged by GSEs	−8,703	−25,652
Provide Authority for Bureau of Engraving and Printing to Construct A New Facility	−318	−579
Require SSN for Child Tax Credit & Earned Income Tax Credit	−5,758	−10,083
Veterans Affairs		
Cap Post–9/11 GI Bill Flight Training at Public Schools	−230	−505
Reinstate COLA Round Down	−749	−2,296
Standardize & Enhance VA Compensation & Pension Benefit Programs	−414	−1,187
Standardize & Improve Veteran Vocational Rehabilitation and Education Benefit Programs	−21	−206
Corps of Engineers		
Divest the Washington Aqueduct	−120	−120
Reform Inland Waterways Financing	−890	−1,780
Office of Personnel Management		
Increase Employee Contributions to 50 Percent of Cost, Phased in at One Percent per Year	−21,379	−68,705
Modify the Government Contribution Rate to Federal Employees Health Benefits Program Premiums	−814	−2,757
Reduce Federal Retirement Benefits	−24,808	−83,725
Other Independent Agencies		
Divest Tennessee Valley Authority Transmission Assets	−3,576	−3,671
Eliminate the Securities and Exchange Commission's Reserve Fund	−158	−408
Enact Spectrum License User Fee	−1,450	−3,950
Reform the Postal Service	−22,662	−44,490
Restructure the Consumer Financial Protection Bureau	−2,772	−6,461

[1] Savings for *Reduce Improper Payments and Other Program Integrity* include $1,494 million in savings that are also included in *Reform Federal Disability Programs* ($579 million over 10 years) and *Medicare: Address Fraud and Abuse* ($915 million over 10 years).

DISCRETIONARY
ELIMINATIONS AND REDUCTIONS

REDUCTION: AGRICULTURAL QUARANTINE INSPECTION USER FEE
Department of Agriculture

The Administration proposes establishing a new discretionary user fee for the Animal and Plant Health Inspection Service (APHIS) Agricultural Quarantine Inspection (AQI) pre-departure program. The fees would recover the full costs of APHIS' inspections of passengers and cargo traveling to the continental United States from Hawaii and Puerto Rico to prevent the introduction of non-native agricultural pests and diseases into the mainland.

Funding Summary
(In millions of dollars)

	2017 Enacted	2019 Request	2019 Change from 2017
Budget Authority..	29	0	-29

Justification

While a user fee is collected from passengers and cargo originating from foreign countries, the expense of AQI for those traveling from Hawaii and Puerto Rico is currently appropriated. Given the significant risks associated with numerous fruits, vegetables, and other plant products from Hawaii and Puerto Rico, APHIS inspects all baggage of passengers leaving these islands. The proposed user fee would fund this inspection program, and allow travelers and businesses to pay for the services they use.

REDUCTION: ANIMAL AND PLANT HEALTH INSPECTION SERVICE
Department of Agriculture

The Administration proposes a reduction to the Animal and Plant Health Inspection Service (APHIS) Salaries and Expenses account to more efficiently use Federal funds while still addressing the highest priority animal and plant health program activities.

Funding Summary
(In millions of dollars)

	2017 Enacted	2019 Request	2019 Change from 2017
Budget Authority...	952	739	-213

Justification

APHIS safeguards the health, welfare, and value of U.S. agricultural and natural resources that are vulnerable to pests, diseases, predation, natural disasters, or inhumane treatment. The proposal would transfer more responsibility for funding animal and plant health programs to the States, local cooperators, and producers that benefit from the programs. The proposal would reduce Federal contributions provided through cooperative agreements in support of State activities, in some cases lowering the Federal cost share responsibility for specific pest and disease programs from about 100 percent down to approximately 50 percent. The proposal would also reduce the appropriated avian health request for the 2019 Budget because APHIS has ample available unobligated funds they may use if needed. Additionally, the proposed reduction includes establishing the new discretionary AQI user fee, discussed further in this section.

REDUCTION: CONSERVATION OPERATIONS
Department of Agriculture

The Budget proposes to reduce conservation operations in an effort to encourage private sector participation in conservation planning.

Funding Summary
(In millions of dollars)

	2017 Enacted	2019 Request	2019 Change from 2017
Budget Authority..	864	669	-195

Justification

Conservation Operations funding provides technical assistance to farmers and ranchers to conserve, maintain, and improve environmental outcomes on their land. For example, this funding can provide resource assessments, conservation practice design, resource monitoring, or follow-up of installed practices, such as improved irrigation devices. However, agricultural conservation planning is not an inherently governmental function. The private sector can provide this service, given uniform planning standards that are established by the Government. Currently the private sector offers planning assistance to farmers to implement precision pesticide and nutrient application, for example, which is evidence that the private sector could also provide technical assistance for conservation planning. When the Government funds technical assistance, it crowds out private sector competition. In the absence of Government funding, the private sector could increase farmers' access to technical assistance.

REDUCTION: ECONOMIC RESEARCH SERVICE
Department of Agriculture

The Budget proposes to streamline the research efforts of the Economic Research Service (ERS), and cut waste by proposing to eliminate low-priority research that is often duplicative of research conducted within the private sector and by non-profits, such as rural sociology and U.S. household consumer expenditures.

Funding Summary
(In millions of dollars)

	2017 Enacted	2019 Request	2019 Change from 2017
Budget Authority..	77	45	-32

Justification

The mission of ERS is to inform and enhance public and private decision making on a broad range of economic and policy issues related to agriculture, food, natural resources, and rural America. ERS also provides statistical indicators that gauge the health of the farm sector. The Budget would largely eliminate ERS' research activities, while still providing adequate staff resources for the Agency to develop the statistics needed to measure economic concepts in a dynamic farm and agricultural sector.

By targeting ERS funding to core, recurring data products, rather than low priority research that is duplicative of research conducted by the private sector and non-profits, the Budget provides a framework to better streamline the Department's statistical functions, leverage administrative efficiencies, and focus on core data products similar to other statistical agencies elsewhere within the Government. Streamlining the ERS mission would make the relationship between ERS and the National Agricultural Statistics Service similar to that of the Census and the Bureau for Economic Analysis (BEA) at the Department of Commerce. BEA uses U.S. Census data to develop additional data products as opposed to conducting social science analysis.

REDUCTION: FEDERAL GRAIN INSPECTION SERVICE USER FEE
Department of Agriculture

The Administration proposes to establish a new user fee to recover the costs of the Federal Grain Inspection Service (FGIS). Entities that receive the benefits from FGIS services should pay for the costs of these programs.

Funding Summary
(In millions of dollars)

	2017 Enacted	2019 Request	2019 Change from 2017
Budget Authority..	20	0	-20

Justification

FGIS programs promote and enforce the United States Grain Standards Act and applicable provisions of the Agricultural Marketing Act of 1946. For about $20 million annually, FGIS identifies, evaluates, and implements new or improved techniques for measuring grain quality. FGIS also establishes and updates testing and grading standards to facilitate the marketing of U.S. grain, oilseeds, and related products; briefs foreign buyers; assesses foreign inspection and weighing techniques; and responds to foreign quality and quantity complaints. FGIS activities enable the smooth and fair trade of grains and oilseeds, which benefits sellers and buyers by ensuring a reliable product, lowering transaction costs, and reducing uncertainty in grain markets. The proposal establishes a new discretionary user fee to recover the full costs of these programs. Entities that receive the direct benefits from FGIS services should pay for the costs of these programs.

ELIMINATION: FOREST SERVICE LAND ACQUISITION
Department of Agriculture

The Budget proposes to eliminate Federal land acquisition funding for the Forest Service to focus available funds on the protection and management of existing lands and assets.

Funding Summary
(In millions of dollars)

	2017 Enacted	2019 Request	2019 Change from 2017
Budget Authority...	56	0	-56

Justification

The proposed budget for the Forest Service focuses limited resources on more effectively managing existing assets and lands. Land acquisition at the Forest Service is a lower priority than maintaining adequate funding for ongoing operations and maintenance of the National Forest System and for Wildland Fire Management programs. The Department of Agriculture's Forest Service already owns 193 million acres, about 30 percent of all Federally-owned land.[1] At a time when the Forest Service has more than $5 billion dollars in deferred maintenance, it needs to focus scarce resources and better manage what it owns before acquiring additional lands.

Citations

[1] Congressional Research Service: *Federal Land Ownership: Overview and Data*, R42346, (March 2017).

ELIMINATION: MCGOVERN-DOLE INTERNATIONAL FOOD FOR EDUCATION
Department of Agriculture

The Budget proposes to eliminate the McGovern-Dole International Food for Education (McGovern-Dole) program, which is duplicative of U.S. Agency for International Development (USAID) programs, and has unaddressed oversight and performance monitoring challenges.

Funding Summary
(In millions of dollars)

	2017 Enacted	2019 Request	2019 Change from 2017
Budget Authority..	202	0	-202

Justification

The program provides for the donation of U.S. agricultural commodities, and associated technical and financial assistance, to carry out preschool and school feeding programs in foreign countries. Research shows that school feeding programs in developing countries are usually high-cost investments with little to no returns, and are usually ineffective in achieving their goal to improve nutrition and learning outcomes. Outcomes are generally measured by weight and height gain, and math performance and intelligence tests, respectively.[1] This is because, while these programs feed children, they have implementation challenges in developing countries and create a substitution effect, meaning children consume less at home once they receive a meal at school. In addition, during the 15-year operation of McGovern-Dole, auditors have found oversight weaknesses as reported by the Government Accountability Office (GAO), independent consultants, and the Department of Agriculture's Office of Inspector General.[2] In the most recent GAO report from 2011, GAO found weaknesses in performance monitoring, program evaluations, and prompt closeout of agreements.[3] Weak performance monitoring cannot accurately show whether program objectives are achieved, and ensure that sustainability is ultimately reached in the communities served, once agreements close. McGovern-Dole funding continues to be duplicative of USAID, which funds nutrition and education programs, and the highest priority food aid programs.

Supporters argue that McGovern-Dole increases U.S. agricultural trade opportunities while supporting U.S. farmers by donating surplus commodities abroad that could otherwise result in lower prices for U.S. farmers domestically. However, the amount of U.S. commodities purchased by McGovern-Dole is a negligible portion of U.S. agricultural production and exports. In 2016, McGovern-Dole spent approximately $54 million on U.S. commodities, roughly 0.01 percent of U.S. agricultural production or 0.04 percent of U.S. agricultural exports.

Supporters will also argue that McGovern-Dole increases enrollment and educational outcomes in developing countries. Although school feeding programs can be configured to increase enrollment, the increased enrollment doesn't generally correlate well with improved attendance or, more importantly, with improved educational outcomes. However, research has shown that small cash payments conditioned on school enrollment tend to produce the same results at a much lower cost.

Citations

[1] The United Nations University, Food and Nutrition Bulletin: *School feeding: Outcomes and Costs,* Vol.30 No. 2, (June 2009).

[2] Morgan Franklin Consulting: *Foreign Agricultural Service – Food for Progress and McGovern Dole Program Assessment,* (September 2013).

[3] Government Accountability Office: *International School Feeding: USDA's Oversight of the McGovern-Dole Food for Education Program Needs Improvement,* (May 2011).

ELIMINATION: RURAL BUSINESS AND COOPERATIVE SERVICE
Department of Agriculture

The Budget proposes to eliminate rural business and cooperative programs given findings that they have failed to meet the program goals, and have been improperly managed.

Funding Summary
(In millions of dollars)

	2017 Enacted	2019 Request	2019 Change from 2017
Budget Authority...	103	0	-103

Justification

The Department of Agriculture's (USDA) Rural Business and Cooperative programs provide loans, loan guarantees, grants, and payments designed to increase economic opportunity in rural America.

Year after year, the Government Accountability Office includes the Rural Business & Cooperative Service (RBS) in its annual report on fragmentation, overlap, and duplication; and USDA's Inspector General found two of the Agency's largest loan and grant programs to be improperly managed.[1,2] These programs have not been able to demonstrate that they meet the broader goals of reducing rural poverty, out-migration, or unemployment. Despite the statutory requirement in the 2014 Farm Bill that requires the Secretary of Agriculture to collect data regarding economic activities created through several RBS grant and loan programs, and to submit a periodic report to the Congress on the findings, the RBS programs still lack program evaluation, so it has not been possible to assess program impact.

The Administration's tax, regulatory, and infrastructure policies are expected to be more effective at improving rural economies and job growth.

Citations

[1] United States Department of Agriculture, Office of Inspector General: *American Recovery and Reinvestment Act - Business and Industry Guaranteed Loans - Phase 3 Audit Report*, 34703-0001-32, (March 2013).

[2] United States Department of Agriculture, Office of Inspector General: *Rural Energy for America Program Audit Report*, 34001-0001-21, (August 2016).

ELIMINATION: RURAL WATER AND WASTEWATER GRANTS
Department of Agriculture

The Budget would provide a $1.2 billion Rural Water and Wastewater direct loan level, but proposes to eliminate the grant component of this program. Coupled with this change is a proposal to increase the population limit served by this program from 10,000 to 20,000. While the Administration believes that the Environmental Protection Agency (EPA) or private sector sources should provide the main funding for this activity, the Department of Agriculture (USDA) financing at the higher population limit can address the remaining gap in available financing for relatively small ($2 million-$5 million range) water infrastructure loans in rural communities.

Funding Summary
(In millions of dollars)

	2017 Enacted	2019 Request	2019 Change from 2017
Budget Authority..	509	0	-509

Justification

USDA's water and wastewater program was created years before any large national program was available to address community water treatment facilities. The key Federal program for water infrastructure financing is EPA's State Revolving Funds (SRFs), and funding small, rural treatment facilities could be handled through the SRFs. Since their creation, the SRFs have been federally capitalized for more than 20 years, totaling nearly $70 billion in Federal investment, and are an available resource for financing rural water treatment facilities. Funding the USDA loan program for small rural areas can address a gap in financing for the very smallest of projects that are between $2 million and $5 million in costs.

ELIMINATION: SINGLE FAMILY HOUSING DIRECT LOANS
Department of Agriculture

The Budget proposes to eliminate funding for the Department of Agriculture's (USDA) rural single family housing direct loan program. USDA will continue to offer home ownership assistance through its single family housing guaranteed loans. Financial markets have become more efficient, which has increased the reach of mortgage credit to borrowers with lower credit qualities and incomes. Utilizing the private banking industry to provide home loans, with a guarantee from the Government, is a more efficient way to deliver this assistance.

Funding Summary
(In millions of dollars)

	2017 Enacted	2019 Request	2019 Change from 2017
Budget Authority..	68	0	-68

Note: Loan Level provided in 2017 was $1 billion.

Justification

Historically, USDA has offered both direct and guaranteed homeownership loans. The direction of Rural Development's single family housing mortgage assistance over the last two decades has been toward guaranteed loans. For example, the single family housing guaranteed loan program has grown from $100 million in 1990 to $24 billion today, while the single family direct loan level has remained at approximately $1 billion. Current mortgage rates are historically low and often result in an average 30-year fixed commercial mortgage rate at or below the average borrower rate for the USDA single family direct loan. Furthermore, rural areas once isolated from easy access to credit have shrunk as broadband internet access and correspondent lending have grown.

Given that graduating to private credit is a goal of the direct loan program, pointing borrowers to commercial credit with a Federal guarantee is a preferred way to achieve the USDA policy goal of providing homeownership opportunities to low-income, rural residents. USDA is now in a position to utilize solely the guarantee program and still achieve the Administration's home ownership goals for rural areas at a lower cost to the taxpayers.

ELIMINATION: ECONOMIC DEVELOPMENT ADMINISTRATION
Department of Commerce

The Budget proposes to eliminate the Economic Development Administration (EDA). EDA's grant programs are duplicative of other economic development programs within the Federal Government, as well as State and local efforts.

Funding Summary
(In millions of dollars)

	2017 Enacted	2019 Request	2019 Change from 2017
Budget Authority...	266	15	-251

Justification

EDA provides Federal assistance grants to communities in support of locally-developed economic plans. Types of projects funded by EDA grants include: small-scale infrastructure project; community planning efforts; and environmental studies.

The proposed elimination of EDA is part of a broader effort to eliminate duplicative and unauthorized economic development programs across the Federal Government. The Congress has not authorized EDA's development assistance grants since the authority expired in 2008.[1] A 2011 Government Accountability Office (GAO) report found that each of the 80 economic development programs at the four departments it reviewed (Departments of Commerce, Housing and Urban Development, Agriculture, and the Small Business Administration) overlapped with at least one of the other programs reviewed.[2]

Multiple administrations have questioned the effectiveness of many of EDA's grant programs. In particular, both the Bush and Obama Administrations proposed to eliminate or drastically reduce EDA's Public Works grant program, which provides small grants with limited impact to localized projects. Additionally, EDA has been cited by both GAO and the Department of Commerce's Office of Inspector General for inconsistent documentation and lack of transparency in the awards process for these programs.[3,4] Despite these concerns, and the requests from administrations of both political parties, the Congress continues to provide funding for EDA and the Public Works grant program, even though they have failed to authorize the program since its authorization expired in 2008.

The Budget provides $15 million to conduct an orderly closure of EDA.

Citations

[1] Congressional Budget Office: *Unauthorized Appropriations and Expiring Authorizations*, (January 2017).

[2] Government Accountability Office: *Efficiency and Effectiveness of Fragmented Economic Development Programs Are Unclear*, GAO-11-477R, (May 2011).

[3] Government Accountability Office: *Documentation of Award Selection Decisions Could Be Improved*, GAO-14-131, (February 2014);

[4] U.S. Department of Commerce, Office of Inspector General: *Economic Development Administration: Financial Assistance Programs' Award Processes Promote Merit-Based Selection Decisions* CFDA Nos. 11.300, 11.303-11.305, and 11.307, Financial Audit Report No. DEN-11580, (December 2000).

ELIMINATION: MANUFACTURING EXTENSION PARTNERSHIP
Department of Commerce

The Budget proposes to eliminate Federal funding for the Manufacturing Extension Partnership (MEP), saving $125 million after accounting for the cost of closing the program. The Administration is seeking to end funding for organizations that duplicate the efforts of other Federal programs, or the non-profit and private sectors. In 2019 the National Institute of Standards and Technology will work to transition MEP centers solely to non-Federal revenue streams, as was intended when the program was first established.

Funding Summary
(In millions of dollars)

	2017 Enacted	2019 Request	2019 Change from 2017
Budget Authority...	130	5	-125

Justification

The Federal MEP program subsidizes advisory and consulting services for small and medium-sized manufacturers through a network of State MEP centers. When the program began, Federal funding for a center was limited to no more than six years to stand up the center, after which the center was intended to transition to entirely non-Federal funding sources. However, many of these MEP centers have been receiving Federal funding for decades, and many of the services provided by MEP centers can be obtained elsewhere.

For many years critics have labeled the MEP program as "corporate welfare" since it provides direct support to industry,[1,2] and the Congressional Budget Office identified the program as suitable for elimination nearly a decade ago.[3]

Citations

[1] United States Senate Committee on Government Affairs: *The Advanced Technology Program and other Corporate Subsidies,* Statement of Stephen Moore, Director of Federal Policy, CATO Institute, (June 3, 1997).

[2] Republican Study Committee: *Fiscal Year 2017 Blueprint for a Balanced Budget 2.0.*

[3] Congressional Budget Office: *Budget Options: Volume 2,* (August 2009).

ELIMINATION: NATIONAL OCEANIC AND ATMOSPHERIC ADMINISTRATION GRANTS AND EDUCATION

Department of Commerce

The Budget proposes to eliminate funding for several lower priority and, in some cases, unauthorized, National Oceanic and Atmospheric Administration (NOAA) grant and education programs, including Sea Grant; the National Estuarine Research Reserve System; Coastal Zone Management Grants; the Office of Education; and the Pacific Coastal Salmon Recovery Fund. These eliminations would allow NOAA to better target remaining resources to core missions and services.

Funding Summary
(In millions of dollars)

	2017 Enacted	2019 Request	2019 Change from 2017
Budget Authority..	273	0	-273

Justification

These grant and education programs generally support State, local, and/or industry interests, and these entities may choose to continue some of this work with their own funding. In addition, these grants often are not optimally targeted, in many instances favoring certain species or geographic areas over others, or distributing funds by formula rather than directing them to programs and projects with the greatest need or potential benefit. NOAA will continue to serve as a resource and provide technical assistance as appropriate on many of the issues funded by these programs. For example, the Budget would continue to provide support for NOAA's Coastal Zone Management and Services program, which makes available science, data, and technical assistance to State, local, and other entities to inform coastal management and development.

ELIMINATION: 21ST CENTURY COMMUNITY LEARNING CENTERS
Department of Education

The Budget proposes to eliminate the 21st Century Community Learning Centers (21st CCLC) program given performance data demonstrates that the program is not achieving its goals. Additionally, Federal, State, local, or private funds, including the $15 billion Title I program could support the provision of 21st CCLC activities.

Funding Summary
(In millions of dollars)

	2017 Enacted	2019 Request	2019 Change from 2017
Budget Authority..	1,192	0	-1,192

Justification

The 21st CCLC program, authorized under the Every Student Succeeds Act of 2015, enables communities to establish or expand centers that provide additional student learning opportunities through before- and after-school programs, and summer school programs, aimed at improving student academic outcomes. While research has demonstrated positive findings on the impact of afterschool programs overall, the subset of afterschool programs funded by 21st CCLC are not, on the whole, helping students meet challenging State academic standards. For example, on average, from 2013 to 2015, less than 20 percent of program participants improved from not proficient to proficient or above on State assessments in reading and mathematics. Additionally, student improvement in academic grades was limited, with States reporting higher math and English grades for less than half of regular program participants. These recent results are consistent with findings of the last rigorous national evaluation of the program, conducted in 2005, which also found the program had limited academic impact.[1] Additionally, nearly 60 percent of students attend 21st CCLC for fewer than 30 days a year, suggesting that the majority of families with participating students do not use the program for childcare.

These data strongly suggest that the 21st CCLC is not generating the benefits commensurate with an annual investment of more than $1 billion in limited Federal education funds. Moreover, the provision of before- and after-school academic enrichment opportunities may be better supported with other Federal, State, local, or private funds, including the $15 billion Title I Grants to Local Educational Agencies program.

Citations

[1] U.S. Department of Education, National Center for Education Evaluation and Regional Assistance: *When Schools Stay Open Late: The National Evaluation of the 21st Century Community Learning Centers Program: Final Report,* (October 2004).

ELIMINATION: COMPREHENSIVE LITERACY DEVELOPMENT GRANTS
Department of Education

The Budget proposes to eliminate the Comprehensive Literacy Development Grants program (formerly known as Striving Readers), given the program has limited impact and duplicates activities that may be supported with other Federal, State, local, and private funds.

Funding Summary
(In millions of dollars)

	2017 Enacted	2019 Request	2019 Change from 2017
Budget Authority..	190	0	-190

Justification

The Comprehensive Literacy Development Grants program makes competitive awards to States to improve literacy instruction from birth through grade 12. The program has limited impact and duplicates activities that may be supported by other sources of both Federal and non-Federal funds. For example, the Title I Grants to Local Educational Agencies program provides over $15 billion to more than 14,000 school districts that may be used to support effective, evidence-based reading instruction. By comparison, the last cohort of Striving Readers grants served only six States and just a handful of districts in each State. Moreover, a 2015 study by the Institute of Education Sciences indicated that a majority (six out of 10) of the interventions implemented by the 2009 and 2006 grant cohorts had no discernible effects on reading achievement.[1] States or school districts that want to test or expand the use of evidence-based literacy instruction may seek funding under the Education Innovation and Research program, which provides grant awards for scaling up effective practices that are comparable in size to those available through the Comprehensive Literacy Development Grants program.

Citations

[1] U.S. Department of Education, National Center for Education Evaluation and Regional Assistance, Institute of Education Sciences: *Summary of Research Generated by Striving Readers on the Effectiveness of Interventions for Struggling Adolescent Readers*, NCEE 2016-4001, (2015).

ELIMINATION: FEDERAL SUPPLEMENTAL EDUCATIONAL OPPORTUNITY GRANTS
Department of Education

The Budget proposes to eliminate the Federal Supplemental Educational Opportunity Grant (SEOG) program, given the program is a less targeted way to deliver need-based grant aid than Pell Grants. Eliminating the program would also reduce complexity in Federal student aid.

Funding Summary
(In millions of dollars)

	2017 Enacted	2019 Request	2019 Change from 2017
Budget Authority..	733	0	-733

Justification

The SEOG program provides need-based grant aid to eligible undergraduate students to help reduce financial barriers to postsecondary education. Currently, SEOG awards are not optimally allocated based on a student's financial need, despite being a need-based program. Although participating institutions must give "priority" in awarding SEOG funds to Pell-eligible students, there is no requirement that the size of these awards be tied to the need of the student. As a result, institutions are given the discretion to provide larger SEOG awards to students that do not exhibit the highest need. In fact, Department of Education data show that the average dependent-student SEOG award in award year 2015-2016 increased as student income levels increased. Furthermore, provisions in the SEOG funding allocation formula also distort the targeting of aid. For example, Department data show that about 69 percent of Pell funding goes to students attending public four-year or public two-year institutions, while only 52 percent of SEOG funds go to these institutions. Moreover, the SEOG program is part of a complex array of Federal aid programs that could benefit from better targeting of aid to needy students. This program's authorization expired in 2014.

REDUCTION: FEDERAL WORK STUDY
Department of Education

The Budget proposes to significantly reduce the Federal Work Study (FWS) program while reforming it to support workforce and career-oriented training opportunities for low-income undergraduate students in order to create pathways to high-paying jobs.

Funding Summary
(In millions of dollars)

	2017 Enacted	2019 Request	2019 Change from 2017
Budget Authority..	990	200	-790

Justification

The FWS program assists needy undergraduate and graduate students in financing postsecondary education costs through part-time employment. However, the program includes outdated provisions in allocating funding and in determining student need that make it inefficient at allocating funds to the neediest students. It is also not well-designed to use the employment as an opportunity to advance students' career and training opportunities. Studies have shown very low rates of students reporting that their FWS jobs are related to their career goals or majors.[1]

According to Department data, dependent students with family incomes at or above $30,000 received 66 percent of FWS funds compared to 33 percent of FWS funds going to students with family incomes below $30,000. Independent students, who typically have lower family incomes, received 47 percent of all Pell Grant aid, but only received 18 percent of FWS funds. This program's authorization expired in 2014.

The Budget would reform the program to both improve its targeting and its ability to provide students with career-oriented training. The program would allocate funds to schools based, in part, on enrollment of Pell recipients. Schools could fund individual students through subsidized employment, paid internships, or other designs provided the placements were career or academically relevant. Schools could also fund broader programs that served multiple students that expose students to or build their preparedness for careers.

Citations

[1] Wisconsin HOPE Lab: *What We're Learning: Work-Study Program A Data Update from the Wisconsin HOPE Lab,* Data Brief 16-06, (October 19, 2016).; Scott-Clayton et al.: *Should student employment be subsidized? Conditional counterfactuals and the outcomes of work-study participation,* Economics of Education Review, 52, 1–18 (2016).

ELIMINATION: GAINING EARLY AWARENESS AND READINESS FOR UNDERGRADUATE PROGRAMS (GEAR UP)
Department of Education

The Budget eliminates Gaining Early Awareness and Readiness for Undergraduate Programs (GEAR UP), consistent with the Administration's belief in reducing the Federal role in education, eliminating duplicative programs, and reallocating scarce Federal resources to higher priority programs. Many of the activities supported under GEAR UP can be supported through the Administration's proposal to transition the Federal TRIO Programs into a consolidated State formula grant program that would support activities - including those authorized under GEAR UP - to help low-income and other disadvantaged students progress through the academic pipeline from middle school through postsecondary.

Funding Summary
(In millions of dollars)

	2017 Enacted	2019 Request	2019 Change from 2017
Budget Authority..	340	0	-340

Justification

GEAR UP provides grants to States to support college preparation and awareness activities to ensure low-income elementary, middle, and secondary students are prepared for and enroll in postsecondary education. The program is authorized by the Higher Education Act (HEA), which has not been reauthorized since the 2008 Higher Education Opportunity Act. Authorization of the HEA technically expired in 2014.

There is limited rigorous evidence that the GEAR UP program is effective, particularly in achieving the program's ultimate objectives of increasing high school graduation and college enrollment rates. For example, although a 2008 evaluation found a positive association between GEAR UP participation and some early outcomes such as increasing students' and parents' knowledge of postsecondary opportunities, and increasing rigorous course-taking, there was no indication of an association with improved grades or school behavior, and the evaluation did not report on high school graduation or college enrollment outcomes.[1]

In addition, many of the activities supported under GEAR UP can be supported through the ESEA Title I grants to States and the Administration's proposal to restructure the Federal TRIO Programs. Under the proposal to transition Federal TRIO programs into a consolidated State formula grant program, the Department of Education would provide funding directly to States to support activities to help low-income and other disadvantaged students progress through the academic pipeline from middle school through postsecondary education. This proposal would shift authority and responsibility from the Federal government to the States; improve alignment between Federal resources and need; invest in activities that are most supported by evidence; and enable the Department to re-allocate limited staff resources from competition-related activities to areas that are critical to help ensure appropriate and effective use of limited taxpayer resources, such as grant monitoring and oversight, performance improvement, and program evaluation. The Administration believes that restructuring the Federal TRIO programs into a single State formula grant program, including incorporating activities authorized under GEAR UP, would yield significant program management efficiencies and support more effective uses of Federal resources.

Citations

[1] U.S. Department of Education, Office of Planning, Evaluation, and Policy Development, Policy and Program Studies Service: *Early Outcomes of the GEAR UP Program: Final Report,* (2008).

ELIMINATION: IMPACT AID PAYMENTS FOR FEDERAL PROPERTY
Department of Education

The Budget proposes to eliminate Impact Aid Payments for Federal Property. These payments compensate school districts for the presence of Federal property, without regard for the presence of federally-connected students, and therefore do not necessarily support the education of federally-connected students, which is the intent of the Impact Aid program.

Funding Summary
(In millions of dollars)

	2017 Enacted	2019 Request	2019 Change from 2017
Budget Authority..	69	0	-69

Justification

The primary purpose of the Impact Aid program is to help pay for the education of federally-connected children, and fund programs that serve federally-connected children. The Payments for Federal Property program compensates school districts for lost property tax revenue due to the presence of Federal lands without regard to whether those districts educate any federally-connected children as a result of the Federal presence. When this authority was established in 1950, its purpose was to provide assistance to local educational agencies (LEAs) in cases where the Federal Government had imposed a substantial and continuing burden by acquiring a considerable portion of real property in the LEA. The law applied only to property acquired since 1938 because, in general, LEAs had been able to adjust to acquisitions that occurred before that time. The Administration believes that the majority of LEAs receiving assistance under this program have now had sufficient time to adjust to the removal of the property from their tax rolls.

ELIMINATION: INTERNATIONAL EDUCATION
Department of Education

The Budget proposes to eliminate the International Education and Foreign Language Studies Domestic and Overseas Programs, which are designed to strengthen the capability and performance of American education in foreign languages and international studies. Other Federal agencies, whose primary missions are national security, implement similar programs and are better equipped to support the objective of these programs.

Funding Summary
(In millions of dollars)

	2017 Enacted	2019 Request	2019 Change from 2017
Budget Authority...	72	0	-72

Justification

Grants are awarded to institutions of higher education to support centers, programs, and fellowships to increase the number of experts in foreign languages and international studies, meet national needs, and strengthen the teaching and research of foreign languages and international education at all levels. While the Administration recognizes the critical need for our Nation to have a readily available pool of international, regional, and advanced language experts for economic, foreign affairs, and national security purposes, it is unclear that this goal is consistent with the Department of Education's core mission. Other Federal agencies, whose primary missions are national security, implement similar programs and are better equipped to support this critical objective. Therefore, the Budget proposes to eliminate these duplicative programs. These programs are authorized by the Higher Education Act (HEA), which has not been reauthorized since the 2008 Higher Education Opportunity Act. Authorization of the HEA expired in 2014.

ELIMINATION: PROMISE NEIGHBORHOODS
Department of Education

The Budget proposes to eliminate the Promise Neighborhoods program as part of an effort to refocus the Department of Education's investments on formula programs that put decision-making power back in the hands of States and local communities. Additionally, Promise Neighborhood activities and interventions could continue to be supported by other Federal, State, and local resources.

Funding Summary
(In millions of dollars)

	2017 Enacted	2019 Request	2019 Change from 2017
Budget Authority..	73	0	-73

Justification

The Promise Neighborhoods program, authorized under the Every Student Succeeds Act of 2015, provides competitive grants that help distressed communities provide students and their families with a continuum of services and support in order to improve academic and developmental outcomes. The Budget proposes eliminating the Promise Neighborhoods program as part of an effort to refocus the Department of Education's investments on formula programs that put decision-making power back in the hands of States and local communities. Additionally, Promise Neighborhood activities and interventions can continue to be supported by other Federal, State, local, and private resources.

ELIMINATION: STATEWIDE LONGITUDINAL DATA SYSTEMS
Department of Education

The Budget proposes to eliminate the Statewide Longitudinal Data Systems (SLDS) program because the program has already successfully completed its mission and is no longer needed to establish Statewide longitudinal data systems.

Funding Summary
(In millions of dollars)

	2017 Enacted	2019 Request	2019 Change from 2017
Budget Authority..	32	0	-32

Justification

The SLDS program provides grants and technical assistance to help States design, develop, and implement Statewide longitudinal data systems to efficiently and accurately manage, analyze, disaggregate, and use individual student data. This program has successfully fulfilled its purpose - 47 States, the District of Columbia, Puerto Rico, the U.S. Virgin Islands, and American Samoa have received awards allowing them to set up longitudinal data systems to answer key questions about education. As States shift from establishing data systems to actually using the data, there is no longer any need for a large Federal investment.

ELIMINATION: STRENGTHENING INSTITUTIONS
Department of Education

The Budget proposes to eliminate funding for the Strengthening Institutions Program (SIP). SIP is authorized by Title III of the Higher Education Act (HEA). Titles III and V of the HEA authorize numerous programs that support Historically Black Colleges and Universities (HBCUs) and Minority-Serving Institutions (MSIs). SIP is duplicative of the other Title III and V programs that provide program funding for institutional support activities. The Budget would preserve funding for programs that support HBCUs, consistent with the President's executive order on HBCUs, and streamline funding for MSIs.

Funding Summary
(In millions of dollars)

	2017 Enacted	2019 Request	2019 Change from 2017
Budget Authority..	87	0	-87

Justification

All of the institutional support activities authorized under SIP are also authorized under other HEA Title III and V programs that provide discretionary and mandatory funding for a wide range of authorized institutional support activities, including strengthening infrastructure and enhancing fiscal stability. Strengthening the quality of educational opportunities in institutions of higher education dedicated to serving low-income and minority students is a critical part of the Administration's efforts to foster more and better opportunities in higher education for communities that are often underserved, as the President asserted in his executive order on HBCUs. Accordingly, the Budget would protect funding for Title III and V programs that support HBCUs and MSIs that specifically serve large numbers of minority students.

SIP and other Title III and V programs are authorized by the Higher Education Act (HEA), which has not been reauthorized since the 2008 Higher Education Opportunity Act. Authorization of the HEA technically expired in 2014.

ELIMINATION: STUDENT SUPPORT AND ACADEMIC ENRICHMENT GRANTS
Department of Education

The Budget proposes to eliminate the Student Support and Academic Enrichment Grants program. The Administration does not believe limited Federal resources should be allocated to this program given that the program allows the funds to be distributed to all school districts that receive Title I, Part A funds, which makes it likely that award amounts will be too small to have a meaningful impact. The funding is also duplicative of other Federal and non-Federal funding, including the $15 billion Title I Grants to Local Educational Agencies (LEA) program.

Funding Summary
(In millions of dollars)

	2017 Enacted	2019 Request	2019 Change from 2017
Budget Authority..	400	0	-400

Justification

The Student Support and Academic Enrichment Grants program, authorized under the Every Student Succeeds Act of 2015, provides funding to school districts for activities that support well-rounded educational opportunities, safe and healthy students, and the effective use of technology. Subgrants can be awarded by formula to all school districts that receive Title I, Part A funds, which at the current funding level of $400 million, would result in award amounts of less than $30,000 for the vast majority of school districts. The Administration does not believe limited Federal resources should be allocated to a program where many of its grants will likely be too small to have a meaningful impact. Furthermore, the school districts that do receive at least $30,000 must follow funding restrictions that prescribe a minimum amount that must be spent on the program's different categories of activities, further diluting the program's impact and removing discretion that is best left to local decision-makers. Also, the activities authorized under this program generally can be supported with funds from other Federal, State, local, and private sources, including similarly flexible funds provided under the $15 billion Title I Grants to LEAs program.

ELIMINATION: SUPPORTING EFFECTIVE INSTRUCTION STATE GRANTS
Department of Education

The Budget proposes to eliminate Supporting Effective Instruction (SEI) State Grants (Title II State grants), a program that provides formula funds to States to improve the quality and effectiveness of teachers, principals, and other school leaders. SEI grants are poorly targeted and funds are spread too thinly to have a meaningful impact on student outcomes. In addition, there is limited evidence that teacher professional development (PD), a primary activity funded by the program, has led to increases in student achievement.

Funding Summary
(In millions of dollars)

	2017 Enacted	2019 Request	2019 Change from 2017
Budget Authority...	2,044	0	-2,044

Justification

The Budget proposes to eliminate the Supporting Effective Instruction (SEI) State Grants program. While the SEI State Grants program authorizes a wide range of activities, in school year 2015-2016, 52 percent of funds were used for PD and 25 percent were used for class-size reduction. A Local Educational Agency that identifies either activity as a key strategy for responding to a comprehensive needs assessment may use Title I, Part A funds for the same purpose. Title I funds also may be used to recruit and retain effective teachers. In addition, PD as currently provided, has shown limited impact on student achievement. For example, a recent evaluation of an intensive elementary school mathematics PD program found that while the PD improved teacher knowledge and led to improvements in teachers' use and quality of explanation in the classroom, there was no difference in student achievement test scores on either the State assessment or on a study-administered math test.[1] Additional Department of Education-funded studies of PD have found similar results.[2,3] While class size reduction has been shown to increase student achievement, school districts used SEI State Grant funds to pay the salaries of an estimated 8,000 teachers in school year 2015-2016, out of a total nationwide teacher workforce of roughly three million teachers. These data suggest that eliminating the program would likely have minimal impact on class sizes or teacher staffing levels.

Citations

[1] Institute of Education Sciences: *Middle School Mathematics Professional Development Impact Study*, (May 2011).

[2] Institute of Education Sciences: *Elementary School Reading Professional Development Impact Evaluation*, (September 2008).

[3] Institute of Education Sciences: *Does Content-focused Teacher Professional Development Work? Findings from Three Institute of Education Sciences Studies*, (November 2016).

ELIMINATION: TEACHER GRANT PROGRAMS
Department of Education

The Budget proposes to eliminate four competitive grant programs intended to increase the number of effective teachers in K-12 schools: Supporting Effective Educator Development (SEED), Teacher and School Leader Incentive Grants (TSLIG), School Leader Recruitment and Support (SLRS), and Teacher Quality Partnerships (TPQ). Given fiscal constraints, elimination of these competitive grant programs will allow the Department to provide strong support for State formula programs, which empower States to select services that are best-suited to address local educational needs.

Funding Summary
(In millions of dollars)

	2017 Enacted	2019 Request	2019 Change from 2017
School Leader Recruitment and Support..	15	0	-15
Supporting Effective Educative Development (SEED)..	65	0	-65
Teacher and School Leader Incentive Grants..	200	0	-200
Teacher Quality Partnership...	43	0	-43

Justification

The SEED program supports competitive grants for evidence-based educator preparation and on-going professional training. The TSLIG program provides competitive grants to help school systems develop and implement human capital management systems or performance-based compensation systems. SLRS provides competitive grants to improve leadership in high-needs schools. The TQP program provides competitive grants to partnerships of school districts and higher education institutions to create a variety of effective pathways into teaching and increase the number of teachers effective in improving student outcomes. These four competitive grant programs have supported the development of evidence-based strategies in the past and funding to support evidence-based professional development activities and training for teachers and school leaders will remain available to States through Elementary and Secondary Education Act formula grant funds (e.g., Title I). States are better-positioned than the Federal government to determine the best strategies to address local teacher workforce needs, and States and other stakeholders may continue to support the efforts of past grantees if they find the strategies to be valuable in addressing their educational challenges.

ELIMINATION: TECHNICAL ASSISTANCE PROGRAMS
Department of Education

The Budget proposes to eliminate two Department of Education technical assistance programs, Regional Educational Laboratories and Comprehensive Centers, because they are underutilized and do not meet the needs of their intended stakeholders.

Funding Summary
(In millions of dollars)

	2017 Enacted	2019 Request	2019 Change from 2017
Comprehensive Centers..	50	0	-50
Regional Education Labs...	54	0	-54

Justification

The Budget proposes eliminating the Regional Educational Laboratories (RELs) program and the Comprehensive Centers program, which provide technical assistance in different ways with the goal of improving education and student achievement. Under the RELs program, laboratories conduct applied research and development; provide technical assistance; develop multimedia educational materials and other products; and disseminate information in an effort to help others use knowledge from research and practice to improve education. Comprehensive Centers help increase State capacity to assist districts and schools in meeting student achievement goals.

In a 2015 evaluation of the RELs that included a nationally representative survey, only 29 percent of State administrators, and 26 percent of district administrators, reported that their research and technical assistance needs were met "very well." Less than half of State administrators, and only 18 percent of district administrators, relied on the REL program "to a great extent" or "to a moderate extent." Many of the REL providers are also Comprehensive Center grantees, and there is little evidence that the Comprehensive Center program increases student achievement in partner districts. Outside of the RELs and Comprehensive Centers, States have access to over a billion dollars in Federal funding (through Every Student Succeeds Act formula grants) that can be used to address their unique technical assistance needs.

Citations

[1] National Center for Education Evaluation and Regional Assistance: *Evaluation of the Regional Educational Laboratories, Final Report,* NCEE 2015 4008, (2015).

ELIMINATION: ADVANCED RESEARCH PROJECTS AGENCY - ENERGY
Department of Energy

The Budget proposes to eliminate the Advanced Research Project Agency-Energy (ARPA-E) program, recognizing the private sector's primary role in taking risks to commercialize breakthrough energy technologies with real market potential.

Funding Summary
(In millions of dollars)

	2017 Enacted	2019 Request	2019 Change from 2017
Budget Authority...	305	0	-305

Justification

ARPA-E is a separate office within the Department of Energy (DOE) that supports energy projects. Appropriations for ARPA-E were only authorized through 2013 under the America COMPETES Reauthorization Act of 2010 (P.L. 111-358). In addition, there has been concern about the potential for ARPA-E's efforts to overlap with Research & Development (R&D) being carried out, or which should be carried out, by the private sector. No new appropriations are requested in 2019. The Department would request reprogramming of prior year unobligated balances for program closeout activities, to ensure full closure of ARPA-E by mid-2020. Any remaining contract closeout and award monitoring activities would be transferred elsewhere within DOE. This proposed elimination reflects both a streamlining of Federal activities and a refocusing on the proper Federal role in energy R&D.

REDUCTION: APPLIED ENERGY PROGRAMS
Department of Energy

The Budget proposes to reduce funding for the Department of Energy's (DOE) applied energy research and development (R&D) programs focused on nuclear, fossil, renewables, efficiency, and electricity. The proposal would focus Federal activities on early-stage R&D, and reflects an increased reliance on the private sector to fund later-stage R&D, including demonstration, commercialization, and deployment where the private sector has a clear incentive to invest.

Funding Summary
(In millions of dollars)

	2017 Enacted	2019 Request	2019 Change from 2017
Non-Defense Budget Authority...	3,776	1,696	-2,080

Justification

The private sector is best positioned and motivated to evaluate the commercial potential of emerging energy technologies and technology advancements relative to the risks of R&D investment. Private sector-led R&D tends to focus on near-term cost and performance improvements where the certainty of profit generation or the prospect of successful market entry are greatest. The Federal role in energy R&D is strongest at the earlier stages, where the greatest motivation is the generation of new knowledge and the proving of novel concepts. In recent years, the applied energy R&D programs have tilted heavily toward subsidizing the later-stage development, demonstration, and commercialization of new energy technologies. The Budget proposes to refocus these programs on energy challenges which present a significant degree of scientific or technical uncertainty across a relatively lengthy time span, making it unlikely that industry would invest in significant R&D on their own. In addition, the DOE-funded applied energy National Laboratories would remain open and operational, while refocusing efforts on early-stage R&D.

Within these proposed reductions, the Budget would eliminate the Weatherization Assistance Program and State Energy Program. This would reduce Federal intervention in State-level energy policy and implementation, and would focus funding for the Office of Energy Efficiency and Renewable Energy on limited, early-stage applied energy R&D.

ELIMINATION: DEPARTMENT OF ENERGY LOAN AND LOAN GUARANTEE PROGRAMS
Department of Energy

The Budget proposes to eliminate the Title XVII Innovative Technology Loan Guarantee Program, the Advanced Technology Vehicle Manufacturing (ATVM) Loan Program, and the Tribal Energy Loan Guarantee Program, because the private sector is better positioned to finance the deployment of commercially viable energy and advanced vehicle manufacturing projects. The Loan Programs Office would continue to conduct monitoring of existing loans.

Funding Summary
(In millions of dollars)

	2017 Enacted	2019 Request	2019 Change from 2017
Title XVII Innovative Technologies, net..	23	7	-16
Advanced Technology Vehicles...	5	1	-4
Tribal Energy...	9	0	-9
Cancellations...	-20	-9	11
Total Budget Authority...	17	-1	-18

Note: In addition to eliminating program management funding, the Budget also proposes to cancel $383 million in unobligated balances from Title XVII and $4.3 billion from ATVM. There are no scoreable savings for these cancellations.

Justification

The Federal role in supporting advanced technologies is strongest in the early stages of research and development. The Government should not be in the business of picking which technologies "win" the commercialization race and displacing private sector investment opportunities. Instead, the Government should recognize the private sector's primary role in taking risks to finance projects in the energy and automobile manufacturing sectors. In addition, the relative inactivity of these programs indicates they are ineffective at attracting borrowers with viable projects who are unable to secure private sector financing. Specifically:

Innovative Technologies—Only three loan guarantees have been closed through this program since its inception, all related to a single project totaling approximately $8 billion. Efforts to increase the attractiveness of the program to potential borrowers have not yielded increased loan activity. The Budget proposes to cancel all remaining loan volume authority. In addition, the Budget proposes to permanently cancel unobligated balances that were appropriated under the American Reinvestment and Recovery Act of 2009 (Public Law 111-5). That Act provided $2.5 billion in credit subsidy for a temporary program to support loan guarantees. This authority has expired, and the unobligated balances are not currently available for new loans. The Budget proposes to cancel $383 million in unobligated credit subsidy while retaining $96 million already set aside to cover the cost of potential modifications.

Advance Technology Vehicles—Since its inception in 2007 only five loans have been closed under this authority, and since 2011 no new loans have closed. Efforts to increase the attractiveness of the program to potential borrowers have not yielded increased loan activity. The Budget proposes to cancel all remaining loan volume authority and appropriated credit subsidy.

Tribal Energy—Originally authorized in 2005, the program was first appropriated funding in 2017. Rules detailing how the program would be implemented have not been promulgated; however, the program authorization is redundant with loan and loan guarantee programs administered by other agencies with missions to serve Tribal entities. The Budget proposes to eliminate this program and cancel all unobligated balances.

ELIMINATION: MIXED OXIDE FUEL FABRICATION FACILITY TERMINATION
Department of Energy

The Budget proposes to terminate the Mixed Oxide (MOX) Fuel Fabrication Facility (MFFF) project and to pursue an alternative disposition method that will achieve significant long-term savings.

Funding Summary
(In millions of dollars)

	2017 Enacted	2019 Request	2019 Change from 2017
MFFF Construction...	335	0	-335
MFFF Termination..	0	220	220
Dilute and Dispose Construction...	0	59	59
Total Budget Authority..	335	279	-56

Justification

The United States began construction of the MFFF in 2007 in accord with the Plutonium Management and Disposition Agreement (PMDA) between the United States and Russia. The goal of the program was to build facilities to dispose of at least 34 metric tons of surplus U.S. weapon-grade plutonium by fabricating it into MOX fuel and irradiating it in commercial nuclear reactors. However, major cost overruns and schedule slippages have led to a re-examination of how best to achieve this goal. Multiple independent analyses confirm that the MOX approach would be significantly more expensive than originally anticipated, and would require approximately $800 million to $1 billion annually for decades. It would be irresponsible to pursue this approach when a far more cost-effective alternative exists.

Due to the project's 350 percent cost growth and 32 year schedule slip, both the Department of Energy and external independent analyses including the U.S. Army Corps of Engineers, have consistently concluded that the MOX approach to plutonium disposition is significantly costlier and would require a much higher annual budget than an alternate disposition method, Dilute and Dispose (D&D). The D&D strategy will disposition surplus U.S. weapon-grade plutonium by diluting with an inert agent and disposing of it at a geologic repository. The termination of the MFFF project and pursuit of D&D would present a significant long-term cost savings, and is projected to take less time to dispose of the plutonium covered under the PMDA.

In 2019, after factoring in termination costs for the MFFF project and pursuing the D&D strategy, this proposal would generate a net cost savings of $56 million compared to the FY 2017 Enacted. Over the life of the project, comparing current cost estimates for the MFFF and D&D, this proposal would avoid up to an additional $10 billion to $12 billion in construction costs and approximately $20 billion more in operating costs while disposing of the surplus plutonium more quickly.

ELIMINATION: AGENCY FOR HEALTHCARE RESEARCH AND QUALITY
Department of Health and Human Services

The Budget proposes to consolidate the Agency for Healthcare Research and Quality's (AHRQ) activities in the National Institutes of Health (NIH). This consolidation would reduce duplication and leverage the expertise of both AHRQ and NIH.

Funding Summary
(In millions of dollars)

	2017 Enacted	2019 Request	2019 Change from 2017
Budget Authority..	324	0	-324

Note: The 2019 NIH Request includes $256 million to consolidate AHRQ activities.

Justification

AHRQ, which has not been authorized since 2005, has had a mandate to enhance the quality, appropriateness, and effectiveness of health services through research and promotion of best practices to improve health systems and outcomes. However, other agencies also conduct health services research and promote best practices that improve delivery of care and enhance patient safety. In particular, NIH already conducts $1.5 billion in health services research, but it is conducted by individual institutes across NIH. Consolidating AHRQ's activities in NIH would reduce duplication and improve the effectiveness of existing health services research by leveraging complementary expertise and allowing research to be disseminated and used more broadly. The Budget proposes to consolidate AHRQ's activities in a new institute in NIH, the National Institute for Research on Safety and Quality, and AHRQ's activities are expected to be further integrated into NIH over time. Though some may argue that consolidating AHRQ will deemphasize health services research, NIH will prioritize important health services research, including research on patient safety and translational research.

ELIMINATION: COMMUNITY SERVICES BLOCK GRANT
Department of Health and Human Services

The Budget proposes to eliminate the Community Services Block Grant (CSBG) because it constitutes a small portion of the funding these grantees receive, and funds are not directly tied to performance, which limits incentives for innovation. CSBG also funds some services that are duplicative of services that are funded through other Federal programs, such as emergency food assistance funded through The Emergency Food Assistance Program (TEFAP) in the Department of Agriculture and workforce programs funded through the Departments of Education and Labor.

Funding Summary
(In millions of dollars)

	2017 Enacted	2019 Request	2019 Change from 2017
Budget Authority..	715	0	-715

Justification

CSBG funds approximately 1,000 nonprofit organizations, local governments, tribal organizations, and migrant and seasonal farm worker organizations commonly referred to as Community Action Agencies (CAAs). CSBG funding is not well targeted, since funding is allocated to States based only on the historical share of funding States received in 1981. Furthermore, funding is distributed by a formula that is not directly tied to performance so it is difficult to ensure funds are spent effectively, which also limits incentives for innovation. CAAs also receive funding from a variety of sources other than CSBG, including from other Federal sources. This program is unauthorized.

ELIMINATION: HEALTH WORKFORCE PROGRAMS
Department of Health and Human Services

The Budget proposes to eliminate health professions training programs that lack evidence of significantly improving the Nation's health workforce. The Budget proposes to continue funding health workforce activities that provide scholarships and loan repayments in exchange for service in areas of the United States where there is a shortage of health professionals.

Funding Summary
(In millions of dollars)

	2017 Enacted	2019 Request	2019 Change from 2017
Budget Authority...	539	88	-451

Justification

The Budget proposes to eliminate funding for 14 health professions training programs that provide funds to training institutions to improve the quantity, quality, diversity, and/or distribution of the Nation's health workforce. These programs have been in existence for decades and most operate under expired authorizations. There is little evidence that these programs significantly improve the Nation's health workforce. For example, less than half of the physician and physician assistant graduates from the Primary Care Training and Enhance Program practice in medically underserved areas.

There are many Federal programs that support the training of health care professionals. A Government Accountability Office report found that four Federal departments, the Departments of Health and Human Services, Veterans Affairs, Defense, and Education, administered 91 programs that supported postsecondary training or education specifically for direct care health professionals.[1]

The Budget would continue to invest in health care workforce activities that directly place health care providers in areas of the country where they are most needed. For example, the Budget would support the NURSE Corps and proposes to extend funding for the National Health Service Corps. These programs provide scholarships or repay educational loans for health professionals that agree to work in areas experiencing a shortage of health care providers.

The Budget proposes a better way to target Federal investments in the healthcare workforce to address provider shortages. To better target Federal spending on graduate medical education (GME) and increase transparency and accountability, the Budget consolidates GME spending in Medicare, Medicaid, and the Children's Hospital GME Payment Program into a new mandatory GME capped grant program. Funding would be distributed to hospitals that are committed to building a strong medical workforce, and would be targeted to address medically underserved communities and health professional shortages.

Citations

[1] Government Accountability Office, Health Care Workforce: *Federal Investments in Training and the Availability of Data for Workforce Projections*, GAO-14-510T, (2014).

ELIMINATION: LOW INCOME HOME ENERGY ASSISTANCE PROGRAM
Department of Health and Human Services

The Budget proposes to eliminate the Low Income Home Energy Assistance Program (LIHEAP) in order to reduce the size and scope of the Federal Government, and better target resources within the Department of Health and Human Services' Administration for Children and Families.

Funding Summary
(In millions of dollars)

	2017 Enacted	2019 Request	2019 Change from 2017
Budget Authority..	3,390	0	-3,390

Justification

LIHEAP is a Federal program that has been known to have sizeable fraud and abuse, leading to program integrity concerns. Specifically, a 2010 Government Accountability Office (GAO) study concluded that the program lacked proper oversight, which resulted in a significant number of improper payments. In particular, the report highlighted a number of incidents in which program funds were distributed to deceased or incarcerated individuals. In addition, the report determined that LIHEAP application processors did little to prevent awards from being provided to individuals with fake addresses and fake energy bills. Since the report, States have taken steps to work toward improving the verification of identify and income.

Perhaps more notably, the Budget recognizes the program is no longer a necessity as States have adopted their own policies to protect constituents against energy concerns. Since LIHEAP was created in 1981, many States have enacted so-called "disconnection policies." In fact, all 50 States and the District of Columbia have imposed regulations that prevent utility companies from disconnecting energy needs from their residents under certain circumstances. In total, 15 of those States enforce temperature restrictions related to freezing and/or extreme heat weather. Other States use date-specific criteria. For example, Minnesota utilizes a "Cold Weather Rule," which requires utility companies to provide electricity and gas during the coldest months, from October 15 until April 15.

Citations

[1] Government Accountability Office, Low-Income Home Energy Assistance Program: *Greater Fraud Prevention Controls Are Needed*, GAO-10-621 (June 2010)

REDUCTION: NATIONAL INSTITUTE FOR OCCUPATIONAL SAFETY AND HEALTH
Department of Health and Human Services

The Budget proposes to fund important research conducted by the National Institute for Occupational Safety and Health (NIOSH), while proposing to eliminate activities that have less of a direct public health impact. The Budget proposes to consolidate the activities and research of NIOSH within the National Institutes of Health (NIH) to improve coordination of research across the Federal Government. Within NIH, NIOSH would continue to support the highest priority occupational safety and health research.

Funding Summary
(In millions of dollars)

	2017 Enacted	2019 Request	2019 Change from 2017
Budget Authority..	335	200	-135

Justification

NIOSH was created within the Centers for Disease Control and Prevention (CDC) in 1970 to ensure safe and healthful working conditions for Americans, including mine safety research. NIOSH is primarily a research agency focused on occupation safety and health, with approximately two-thirds of its activities funding intramural research. The Budget prioritizes core public health activities and proposes to reduce programs that have less of a direct public health impact, such as some of NIOSH's activities. The Budget proposes to eliminate the Education and Research Centers (ERCs) and other activities where NIOSH does not have enforcement action, or where the private sector or other Federal partners could more effectively conduct these activities. The ERCs were created in the 1970s to develop occupational health and safety training programs in academic institutions. Almost 50 years later, the majority of schools of public health include coursework, and many academic institutions have developed specializations in these areas. The Budget would stop direct Federal funding to support academic salaries, stipends, and tuition and fee reimbursements for occupational health professionals at universities. Some activities conducted by NIOSH could be more effectively conducted by the private sector. For example, NIOSH collects and quantifies human body size and the shape of various occupational groups to develop equipment designs for worker protection. The private sector also conducts similar research in the development of ergonomic equipment.

The Budget's NIOSH proposal reflects the President's effort to reorganize the Government to improve efficiency, effectiveness, and accountability. As part of that, the Budget would consolidate the highest priority occupational safety and health research, and activities of NIOSH, within NIH to improve coordination of research across the Federal Government. As the Nation's leading health research agency, NIH would continue the most important research of NIOSH, including research on mining safety, personal protective technology, and NIOSH's role as mandated under Energy Employees Occupational Illness Compensation Program Act. The World Trade Center Health Program, currently administered by NIOSH, would continue to be administered by the CDC.

REDUCTION: OFFICE OF THE NATIONAL COORDINATOR FOR HEALTH INFORMATION TECHNOLOGY
Department of Health and Human Services

The Budget proposes to restructure the Office of the National Coordinator for Health Information Technology (ONC) by reducing its budget by 36 percent and focusing resources on the highest health information technology (IT) priorities.

Funding Summary
(In millions of dollars)

	2017 Enacted	2019 Request	2019 Change from 2017
Budget Authority...	60	38	-22

Justification

ONC is the principal Federal entity charged with coordinating nationwide efforts to implement and use the most advanced health IT and the electronic exchange of health information. When ONC was created, a small minority of physicians and hospitals used health IT. Now that the vast majority of physicians and hospitals have adopted electronic health records through Federal incentive payments, it is time for a renewed, more focused role for ONC. A restructured ONC would maintain a focus on core health IT functions, such as policy development and coordination, and standards and certification activities. The Budget would eliminate or significantly reduce lower-priority activities, and those activities that can be performed by other entities. For example, the Budget proposes to eliminate the Health IT Adoption portfolio, since 86 percent of physicians and 95 percent of hospitals eligible for the Medicare and Medicaid EHR Incentive Program have adopted EHRs. The Budget would also reduce administrative costs. These changes would improve ONC's ability to be an effective coordinator of nationwide health IT activities and increase the Agency's efficiencies.

REDUCTION: FLOOD HAZARD MAPPING AND RISK ANALYSIS PROGRAM
Department of Homeland Security

The Budget proposes reducing the discretionary appropriation for the National Flood Insurance Program's Flood Hazard Mapping Program. The Budget proposes the reduction to preserve resources for the Department of Homeland Security's core missions.

Funding Summary
(In millions of dollars)

	2017 Enacted	2019 Request	2019 Change from 2017
Budget Authority	178	100	-78

Justification

The Federal Emergency Management Agency (FEMA) maintains quality flood hazard information and develops Flood Insurance Rate Maps (FIRMs, or flood maps). Flood maps communicate flood risks to communities and residents, inform local floodplain management regulations, help communities set minimum floodplain and building standards, determine who is required to purchase flood insurance, and help FEMA to accurately price flood insurance.

FEMA has mapped 1.13 million stream miles covering 98 percent of the population in the United States. However, maintaining maps is an ongoing, resource-intensive effort. With 65 percent of the mapped miles up-to-date, the mapping cycle requires not just continued financial investment, but also process and technology improvements to increase its efficiency.

Given limited resources and the backlog of flood mapping needs despite regular federal investment, the Budget proposes to reduce flood map funding to preserve resources for the Department of Homeland Security's core missions. Over the next year, the Administration will work to improve efficiency in the flood mapping program, including incentivizing increased State and local government investments in updating flood maps to inform land use decisions and reduce risk.

FEMA also collects revenue for mapping under an offsetting collection discretionary account.

ELIMINATION: TRANSPORTATION SECURITY ADMINISTRATION LAW ENFORCEMENT GRANTS
Department of Homeland Security

The Budget proposes to eliminate funding that incentivizes State and local law enforcement entities to provide law enforcement at airports by partially reimbursing those entities. This incentive is no longer necessary nearly 17 years after the September 11, 2001 attacks, as State and local jurisdictions have had plenty of time to adjust and reprioritize resources.

Funding Summary
(In millions of dollars)

	2017 Enacted	2019 Request	2019 Change from 2017
Budget Authority...	45	0	-45

Justification

The Transportation Security Administration provides assistance to State and local law enforcement jurisdictions to partially reimburse law enforcement activity currently at airports. The program was created to encourage law enforcement presence at airports in the wake of the September 11, 2001 attacks, and to lessen the burden on State and local jurisdictions as they refocused law enforcement efforts. In the more than 16 years since those attacks, airport security continues to be a high priority not just for the Federal government, but also for the State and local communities whose economies benefit from aviation.

The amount of financial support offered by this program has waned in recent years, declining below 50 percent of total State and local law enforcement costs in 2016 and continuing to decline. As such, State and local jurisdictions are supporting much more of the cost of providing law enforcement presence at airports. Discontinuing this program would not place an undue burden on State and local jurisdictions, since they already pay the majority of law enforcement costs.

ELIMINATION: CHOICE NEIGHBORHOODS
Department of Housing and Urban Development

The Budget proposes to cancel unobligated balances for the Choice Neighborhoods (Choice) program, recognizing a greater role for State and local governments and the private sector to address community revitalization needs.

Funding Summary
(In millions of dollars)

	2017 Enacted	2019 Request	2019 Change from 2017
Program Level..	138	0	-138
Cancellation...	0	-138	-138
Total Budget Authority..	138	-138	-276

Note: The proposed cancellation reflected includes $137 million from Choice Neighborhoods and $1 million from its predecessor program, HOPE VI.

Justification

Choice provides competitive planning and implementation grants to improve neighborhoods with distressed public and/or assisted housing. In addition to providing a direct investment, this unauthorized program leverages additional private and public funds.[1] While leveraging private resources is desirable, early reports suggest that many of the funds leveraged by Choice grantees were existing commitments and appear as if they would have occurred in the absence of a Choice grant.[2] Furthermore, an early evaluation suggests that Choice grants catalyzing additional resources beyond housing finance, like infrastructure or safety resources needed for neighborhood improvement, were infrequent.[3] The grantees only leveraged additional investments of two to 20 percent of their total grants as a result of Choice designation.

State and local governments may be better positioned to fund locally-driven strategies for neighborhood revitalization. Moreover, local government's commitment to policy changes and interagency coordination are critical to achieving the educational and public safety goals associated with the program, and to achieve the necessary scale to impact entire neighborhoods.[3]

Citations

[1] U.S. Department of Housing and Urban Development: *Choice Neighborhoods 2015 Grantee Report*, (January 2016).

[2] U.S. Department of Housing and Urban Development: *Developing Choice Neighborhoods: An Early Look at Implementation in Five Sites*, (September 2013).

[3] U.S. Department of Housing and Urban Development: *Choice Neighborhoods: Baseline Conditions and Early Progress*, (September 2015).

ELIMINATION: COMMUNITY DEVELOPMENT BLOCK GRANT
Department of Housing and Urban Development

The Budget proposes to eliminate funding for the Community Development Block Grant (CDBG) program. The program is not well-targeted to the neediest populations and has not demonstrated a measurable impact on communities.

Funding Summary
(In millions of dollars)

	2017 Enacted	2019 Request	2019 Change from 2017
Budget Authority...	3,000	0	-3,000

Justification

CDBG provides flexible formula funds to 1,250 State and local grantees to support a wide range of community and economic development activities (e.g., housing rehabilitation, blight removal, infrastructure and public improvements, and public services). The Federal Government has spent over $150 billion on CDBG since its inception in 1974, but evaluations have been unable to demonstrate program results. The broad purpose and flexible nature of this program allows for a wide range of community activities to be supported, but it is this same flexibility that creates challenges to measuring the program's impact and efficacy in improving communities. The Department of Housing and Urban Development (HUD) Inspector General audits regularly find CDBG grantees did not follow HUD requirements.

The program has also largely remained unchanged since it was last reauthorized in 1994. Studies have shown that the allocation formula poorly targets funds to the areas of greatest need, and many aspects of the program have become outdated.[1] For example, the age of a city's housing stock features prominently in the formula, regardless of its condition, providing more dollars for older, wealthier cities with historic homes than fast-growing cities with similar community development needs. These cities have the fiscal capacity to fund directly or leverage philanthropic dollars for the full range of activities that are supported by CDBG, from street paving to improving parks and recreation facilities. Moreover, decreasing appropriations combined with an increasing number of localities qualifying for CDBG allocations has reduced the size of the individual grants over time, further diluting its impact.

The Budget recognizes that State and local governments are better positioned to address local community and economic development needs.

Citations

[1] Housing Policy Debate: *CDBG at 40: Its Record and Potential,* Volume 24, Issue 1, (2014).

REDUCTION: GRANTS TO NATIVE AMERICAN TRIBES AND ALASKA NATIVE VILLAGES
Department of Housing and Urban Development

The Budget proposes to reduce overall Department of Housing and Urban Development (HUD) funding targeted to Native American Tribes and Alaskan Native villages. The Budget proposes $600 million for the Native American Housing Block Grant (NAHBG) program, and redirects the savings to higher priority areas. The Budget also proposes to eliminate the Indian Community Development Block Grant (ICDBG), which is duplicative of other Federal programs and initiatives.

Funding Summary
(In millions of dollars)

	2017 Enacted	2019 Request	2019 Change from 2017
Native American Housing Block Grant	654	600	-54
Indian Community Development Block Grant	60	0	-60
Total Budget Authority	714	600	-114

Justification

NAHBG provides formula grants to Native American Tribes and Alaska Native villages (Tribes) for affordable housing and related activities. The Budget proposes that funding for this unauthorized program be reduced and redirected to programs in higher priority areas, such as national security and public safety. While the program is fulfilling its mission by increasing the stock of affordable housing in Indian Country, improved data collection is necessary to assess grantee performance on efficiency metrics, such as whether grantees are keeping vacancies to a minimum or turning vacant units over quickly.

ICDBG provides competitive grants to Tribes for a range of projects, including the construction and rehabilitation of affordable housing, community facilities, and infrastructure. The Budget proposes to eliminate ICDBG as it is unauthorized and duplicates, in part, HUD's larger NAHBG program and other Federal programs.

ELIMINATION: HOME INVESTMENT PARTNERSHIPS PROGRAM
Department of Housing and Urban Development

The Budget proposes to eliminate the HOME Investment Partnerships Program, recognizing a greater role for State and local governments and the private sector in addressing affordable housing needs.

Funding Summary
(In millions of dollars)

	2017 Enacted	2019 Request	2019 Change from 2017
Budget Authority..	950	0	-950

Justification

The HOME Investment Partnerships Program provides flexible formula grants to 600 States and localities to expand the supply of affordable housing for low-income households, yet remains unauthorized since 1994. Despite the program's goals and funding, the challenge of affordable housing has only continued to worsen.

Complex market dynamics, including stagnant incomes and local regulations that create barriers to housing development, all contribute to housing cost burden for households across the country, and the problem cannot be solved by the Federal Government or the subsidization of housing construction alone. Moreover, the current system for funding affordable housing is fragmented with varying rules and regulations that create overlap and inefficiencies, as well as challenges to measuring collective performance.[1] The Administration proposes to devolve affordable housing activities to State and local governments who are better positioned to comprehensively address the array of unique market challenges, local policies, and impediments that lead to housing affordability problems.

Citations

[1] Government Accountability Office: *Affordable Rental Housing: Assistance Is Provided by Federal, State, and Local Programs, but There Is Incomplete Information on Collective Performance*, GAO-15-645, (September 2015).

REDUCTION: RENTAL ASSISTANCE PROGRAMS
Department of Housing and Urban Development

The Budget proposes legislative reforms to reduce costs across the Department of Housing and Urban Development's (HUD) rental assistance programs. The proposed policies include increased local control for grantees and administrative simplification, as well as policies that encourage work and self-sufficiency, including increased tenant rent contributions.

Funding Summary
(In millions of dollars)

	2017 Enacted	2019 Request	2019 Change from 2017
Budget Authority...	38,098	33,816	-4,282

Justification

HUD's rental assistance programs (Housing Choice Vouchers, Public Housing, Project-Based Rental Assistance, and Housing for the Elderly and Persons with Disabilities) provide housing subsidies for about 4.7 million very low-income households. These rental assistance programs generally comprise about 80 percent of HUD's total budget. Due to market rent inflation, program costs increase by about three percent every year simply to assist roughly the same number of households. Given current fiscal constraints, this growth is not sustainable.

The Budget proposes fundamental rent reforms across HUD's rental assistance programs. These reforms include increasing tenant rent contributions and minimum rents, reducing the frequency of income recertification, and allowing communities to design programs that address local needs. In the first significant change to tenant rent structures since 1981, the Budget would increase the amount of rent paid by tenants from 30 percent of adjusted income to 35 percent of gross income for all work-able households, but would mitigate this increase for the elderly and persons with disabilities. For those tenants who, in certain circumstances, are unable to pay their rents, the Budget also includes a hardship exemption. These reforms would reduce Federal costs and put the programs on a more sustainable fiscal path, as well as encourage work and simplify program administration.

In addition to the proposed rent reforms, the Budget reduces the overall Federal footprint of housing assistance. While continuing to assist current residents, the Budget proposes to decrease the Public Housing portfolio through locally determined options, including strategically releasing certain housing assets to local control. In this effort, the Federal Government recognizes the need for greater contributions from State and local governments and the private sector to help address affordable housing needs for low-income families.

ELIMINATION: SELF-HELP AND ASSISTED HOMEOWNERSHIP OPPORTUNITY PROGRAM ACCOUNT
Department of Housing and Urban Development

The Budget proposes to eliminate funding for small grant programs that are duplicative or overlap with other Federal, State, and local efforts. The Budget also recognizes a greater role for State and local governments, and the private sector, in addressing community development and affordable housing needs.

Funding Summary
(In millions of dollars)

	2017 Enacted	2019 Request	2019 Change from 2017
Budget Authority..	54	0	-54

Justification

The Budget proposes to eliminate the programs in the Self-Help and Assisted Homeownership Opportunity Program (SHOP) account, including SHOP; Capacity Building for Community Development and Affordable Housing program (Section 4); and the rural capacity building program. These programs represent a small fraction of the funds provided by other Federal, State, local, and private entities to support housing and community development activities. The non-profit organizations that receive these grants should have the capacity to substitute funding through more flexible funding from the private sector and philanthropy. For example:

SHOP—SHOP is a competitive grant program that provides funds to non-profit organizations to assist low-income homebuyers willing to contribute "sweat equity" toward the construction of their homes. This unauthorized program expired in 2001, and the Budget proposes redirecting its funding to other, higher priority activities.

Section 4—Section 4 funding was last authorized in 1996, and the program is effectively an earmark for three organizations. The rural capacity building program is also unauthorized. The Department of Housing and Urban Development has adopted a more integrated and efficient approach to technical assistance and strengthening grantees in recent years, and will align these programs' activities with those efforts, as appropriate.

ELIMINATION: ABANDONED MINE LAND GRANTS
Department of the Interior

The Budget proposes to eliminate funding introduced in 2016 for grants to Appalachian States for economic development projects in conjunction with coal abandoned mine land (AML) reclamation. These grants exceed the mission of the Office of Surface Mining Reclamation and Enforcement (OSMRE), and overlap with existing mandatory funds to reclaim abandoned coal mines.

Funding Summary
(In millions of dollars)

	2017 Enacted	2019 Request	2019 Change from 2017
Budget Authority..	105	0	-105

Justification

The discretionary AML grant program was developed by the Congress in response to the prior administration's 2016 Budget mandatory grant proposal to disburse $1 billion from the unappropriated balance of the AML Fund to expedite the cleanup and redevelopment of eligible lands and waters affected by historic coal mining practices, and thus promote economic development. The Congress subsequently appropriated $90 million in 2016 discretionary funding for these activities in three Appalachian States (Kentucky, West Virginia, and Pennsylvania). OSMRE's expertise is in coal mine reclamation and not economic development. These grants are not central to OSMRE's mission and overlap with more than $300 million in existing 2019 mandatory funds to reclaim abandoned coal mines. The Administration plans to help coal country by streamlining permit approvals and eliminating unnecessary regulations, such as lifting the moratorium on coal leasing on public lands, rolling back the Clean Power Plan, and helping to nullify the Stream Protection Rule.

ELIMINATION: CENTENNIAL CHALLENGE FUND
Department of the Interior

The Budget proposes to eliminate $20 million in discretionary funding for the Centennial Challenge Fund at the National Park Service (NPS). The program provides Federal funding to match donations for signature NPS projects and has primarily been used to fund deferred maintenance projects. This discretionary funding duplicates the existing mandatory funds provided through the 2016 National Park Service Centennial Act, and new mandatory funds for NPS deferred maintenance projects proposed in the Budget through the Public Lands Infrastructure Fund.

Funding Summary
(In millions of dollars)

	2017 Enacted	2019 Request	2019 Change from 2017
Budget Authority...	20	0	-20

Justification

The Budget proposes up to $18 billion over 10 years in mandatory funding for a new Public Lands Infrastructure Fund to help the Department of the Interior (DOI) pay for repairs and improvements to facilities in national parks and on other public lands, which have over $12 billion in deferred maintenance. This new proposal diminishes the need for the Centennial Challenge Fund, which historically has been used primarily to help pay for infrastructure improvement projects. The NPS Centennial was celebrated over three years ago, and limited discretionary resources require DOI to prioritize the funding for other higher-priority activities, such as park operations.

REDUCTION: FEDERAL LAND ACQUISITION
Department of the Interior

The Budget proposes to reduce Federal land acquisition funding for the Department of the Interior (DOI) to $8 million, which includes canceling $25 million in prior year balances. This would allow DOI to focus available funds on the protection and management of existing lands and assets.

Funding Summary
(In millions of dollars)

	2017 Enacted	2019 Request	2019 Change from 2017
Budget Authority..	154	8	-146

Note: The FY 2019 Request includes -$25 million in prior year balance cancellations.

Justification

The Budget proposes a reduction of $146 million for Federal land acquisition through DOI. These proposed reductions reflect the Agency's priority to focus available budget resources on maintaining current lands rather than acquiring additional lands. DOI already owns roughly 500 million acres of Federal land. At a time when the Agency has billions of dollars in deferred maintenance, land acquisitions are lower priority activities than maintaining ongoing operations and maintenance.

ELIMINATION: HERITAGE PARTNERSHIP PROGRAM
Department of the Interior

Through the Heritage Partnership Program, the Congress has established 49 National Heritage Areas to commemorate, conserve, and promote areas that include important natural, scenic, historic, cultural, and recreational resources. The Budget proposes to eliminate $19.5 million in funding for the Heritage Partnership Program, which is only partially authorized and is secondary to the primary mission of the National Park Service (NPS). This program provides financial and technical assistance to congressionally designated National Heritage Areas, which are managed by non-Federal organizations to promote the conservation of natural, historic, scenic, and cultural resources. The Budget does include a request for minimal resources to close-out and transition the program to the State, local, or private entities that manage the Areas.

Funding Summary
(In millions of dollars)

	2017 Enacted	2019 Request	2019 Change from 2017
Budget Authority..	20	0	-20

Justification

National Heritage Areas are not part of the National Park System, and the lands are not federally owned and managed. The lands within heritage areas tend to remain in State, local, or private ownership. Thus, these grants to State and local entities are not clearly a Federal responsibility and are therefore a lower priority. Instead, National Heritage Area managers should use the national designation to open doors to more sustainable funding opportunities from local and private beneficiaries. As noted in a Government Accountability Office report, there is no systematic process for designating Heritage Partnership Areas or determining their effectiveness.[1] The proposed funding elimination would also allow the NPS to focus resources on core park and program operations.

Citations

[1] Barry T. Hill, Director, Natural Resources and Environment, U.S. General Accounting Office: *National Park Service: A More Systematic Process for Establishing National Heritage Areas and Actions to Improve Their Accountability Are Needed*, testimony before the Committee on Energy and Natural Resources, U.S. Senate, GAO-04-593T, (March 30, 2004).

ELIMINATION: NATIONAL WILDLIFE REFUGE FUND
Department of the Interior

The Budget proposes to eliminate discretionary funding for the National Wildlife Refuge Fund. This Fund was intended to compensate communities for lost tax revenue from Federal land acquisitions, but fails to take into account the economic benefits refuges provide to communities.

Funding Summary
(In millions of dollars)

	2017 Enacted	2019 Request	2019 Change from 2017
Budget Authority...	13	0	-13

Justification

Though the National Wildlife Refuge Fund was intended to compensate communities for lost tax revenue from Federal land acquisitions, evidence shows that refuges often generate tax revenue for communities, in excess of what was lost, by increasing property values and creating tourism opportunities for the American public to connect with nature. A 2013 study found that National Wildlife Refuges generated an estimated $2.4 billion in sales for local economies, supported over 35,000 jobs, and resulted in over $340 million in tax revenues at the local, State, and Federal level from recreational spending.[1] A study by North Carolina State University in 2012 found that property values surrounding refuges are higher than equivalent property values elsewhere.[2] In addition, approximately $8 million per year in mandatory appropriations is provided to communities from the National Wildlife Refuge Fund.

Citations

[1] U.S. Fish and Wildlife Service: *Banking on Nature: the Economic Benefits to Local Communities of National Wildlife Refuge Visitation,* (October 2013).

[2] North Carolina State University Center for Environmental and Resource Economic Policy: *Amenity Values of Proximity to National Wildlife Refuges,* (April 2012).

REDUCTION: COPS HIRING PROGRAM
Department of Justice

The Budget proposes to reduce resources for the COPS Hiring Program in order to reallocate funding to higher priority Federal law enforcement programs that lead efforts to address gangs, violent crime, and the opioid epidemic in communities across the Nation.

Funding Summary
(In millions of dollars)

	2017 Enacted	2019 Request	2019 Change from 2017
Budget Authority..	195	99	-96

Justification

In 1994, the Clinton Administration began administering the COPS Hiring Program, which was initially designed as a six year program that would enable State and local law enforcement agencies to hire or redeploy 100,000 officers for community policing efforts. The program continues today by subsidizing routine functions of local police departments by funding a portion of entry-level salaries and benefits for newly hired or rehired police officers. These resources are spread thin and are not well targeted to achieve public safety outcomes. For example, the majority of 2017 awards funded only one to two positions per law enforcement agency. Reallocating resources from COPS Hiring to Federal law enforcement allows the Department of Justice (DOJ) to focus on high priority Federal investigations that target criminals posing the greatest threat to society. The Budget provides $14 billion to Federal law enforcement agencies, including the Federal Bureau of Investigation; the Drug Enforcement Administration; the United States Marshals Service; the Bureau of Alcohol, Tobacco, Firearms, and Explosives; and the Organized Crime and Drug Enforcement Task Forces, which work in concert with State and local law enforcement partners. This proposed funding level represents an increase of 2.4 percent over the 2017 Enacted level, and would support DOJ's ability to respond to national security crises; investigate violent- and drug-related crime; and apprehend, detain, and prosecute offenders.

ELIMINATION: STATE CRIMINAL ALIEN ASSISTANCE PROGRAM
Department of Justice

The Budget proposes to eliminate the State Criminal Alien Assistance Program (SCAAP) from the Office of Justice Programs within the Department of Justice. SCAAP, which reimburses State, local, and tribal governments for prior year costs associated with incarcerating certain illegal criminal aliens, is unauthorized and poorly targeted. The Administration proposes to instead invest in border enforcement and border security initiatives that will more effectively address the public safety threats posed by criminal aliens.

Funding Summary
(In millions of dollars)

	2017 Enacted	2019 Request	2019 Change from 2017
Budget Authority..	210	0	-210

Justification

This program represents a general revenue transfer to States that neither focuses resources on immigration enforcement nor fully reimburses their detention costs. In 2016, the reimbursement rate was about 17 cents on the dollar, with just four States – California, Florida, New York, and Texas – receiving over two-thirds of available funds. Further, the program has no performance metrics or programmatic requirements associated with the funds to improve public safety. The program does not require recipients to use SCAAP awards solely for the purpose of addressing the cost of detaining criminal aliens in State, local, and tribal detention facilities. Further, the program does not require States to cooperate with Federal immigration detainer requests, and therefore cannot be leveraged to maximize public safety benefits.

REDUCTION: BUREAU OF INTERNATIONAL LABOR AFFAIRS
Department of Labor

The Budget proposes to eliminate the Department of Labor's international labor grants and reduce International Labor Affairs Bureau (ILAB) staff, instead focusing ILAB on ensuring that U.S. trade agreements are fair for American workers.

Funding Summary
(In millions of dollars)

	2017 Enacted	2019 Request	2019 Change from 2017
Budget Authority...	86	19	-67

Justification

Despite its role in ensuring that U.S. trade agreements are fair for American workers, ILAB spends almost 70 percent of its budget on grants to combat child labor and promote worker rights overseas. Many of these grants are awarded noncompetitively, and while ILAB has funded some impact evaluations of its child labor projects, the findings have been mixed. The completed child labor impact evaluations show that education projects had limited effects on withdrawing and preventing children from participating in child labor.[1] The Budget proposes to eliminate these grants and focus ILAB on ensuring that American workers are competing on a level playing field with other countries.

Citations

[1] Government Accountability Office: *International Labor Grants: DOL's Use of Financial and Performance Monitoring Tools Needs to be Strengthened*, GAO-14-832, (September 2014).

ELIMINATION: INDIAN AND NATIVE AMERICAN PROGRAM
Department of Labor

The Budget proposes to eliminate the Indian and Native American Program (INAP), an unproven program that has never been rigorously evaluated. As an alternative, the Budget would create a Native American set-aside in the Workforce Innovation and Opportunity Act (WIOA) Adult formula grant program, as exists in the WIOA Youth program, bringing Native American training efforts fully into the core workforce system instead of supporting parallel efforts.

Funding Summary
(In millions of dollars)

	2017 Enacted	2019 Request	2019 Change from 2017
Budget Authority...	50	0	-50

Justification

INAP seeks to help low-income and unemployed Native Americans, Native Alaskans, and Native Hawaiians obtain skills necessary to compete in the economy. The program runs competitions through which it gives grants to Indian Tribes, tribal organizations, and other Indian-controlled organizations to provide a wide range of training and support services. Performance results are comparable to the outcomes of Native American participants in the WIOA Adult program, but the INAP program is a more expensive intervention, which calls into question its cost effectiveness. Additionally, there is very little turnover in grantees. The grantee cohort has remained almost exactly the same over the past decade, leading to a situation where grantees are not pushed to improve their performance. The Budget proposes to eliminate standalone funding for this unproven program, instead creating a Native adult set-aside within the WIOA Adult program in order to bring the provision of workforce services to Native American adults into the core workforce system.

REDUCTION: JOB CORPS
Department of Labor

The Budget proposes to reform Job Corps by closing low-performing centers, piloting new approaches to service delivery, and focusing the program on youth most likely to benefit from the intervention. The Budget also proposes to end the U.S. Department of Agriculture's (USDA) role in the program, given that workforce development is not a core part of the Agency's mission.

Funding Summary
(In millions of dollars)

	2017 Enacted	2019 Request	2019 Change from 2017
Budget Authority...	1,704	1,297	-407

Justification

Job Corps provides training and educational services to approximately 50,000 disadvantaged youth (ages 16-24) at 125 primarily residential centers nationwide. The program has historically struggled with numerous issues, including safety and security, uneven center performance, and a lack of innovation. A randomized control trial of the program conducted from 1993-2006 found no overall long-term employment or earnings impacts associated with program participation, though it did find positive long-term earnings impacts for the 20-24 year old cohort.[1]

The Budget proposes aggressive steps to improve Job Corps for the youth it serves by closing centers that chronically do a poor job educating and preparing students for jobs, focusing the program on the older youth for whom it is more effective, improving center safety, and making other changes to sharpen program quality and efficiency. As part of this effort, the Budget is proposing to end USDA's role in the program. Providing workforce development services to disadvantaged youth is not the USDA's core mission or competency, and its 26 centers are disproportionately represented at the bottom of the performance rankings. The Department of Labor (DOL) would also take several administrative steps to improve the quality of the services delivered through the Job Corps program. DOL would shift the outreach and admissions function of the program from private contractors to States, which under the workforce system are already responsible for connecting individuals to jobs and services. The Department would also launch several pilots to test new models for operating Job Corps centers, including through the use of cooperative agreements with non-profits that have expertise in youth development. These reforms would save money by eliminating ineffective centers and finding better ways to educate and train youth.

Citations

[1] Schochet, et al.: *National Job Corps Study: Findings Using Administrative Earnings Record Data,* (2003).

ELIMINATION: MIGRANT AND SEASONAL FARMWORKER TRAINING
Department of Labor

The Budget proposes to eliminate the Migrant and Seasonal Farmworker Training program (also known as the National Farmworker Jobs Program). The program is duplicative in that it creates a parallel training system for migrant and seasonal farmworkers, despite the fact that these individuals are eligible to receive services through the core Workforce Innovation and Opportunity Act (WIOA) formula programs.

Funding Summary
(In millions of dollars)

	2017 Enacted	2019 Request	2019 Change from 2017
Budget Authority..	82	0	-82

Justification

The Migrant and Seasonal Farmworker Training program provides grants to 52 organizations to provide training, employment, and other services to migrant farmworkers, with the goal of increasing their employment and earnings. The program also awards housing assistance grants to 11 organizations. While the program reports favorable performance results in terms of the share of participants entering employment, the program has not been rigorously evaluated so it is unclear whether these outcomes would have happened in the absence of the program. Those participants who currently receive training and employment services are eligible for similar services through the core WIOA Titles I and III formula programs.

In addition, while grants are competitively awarded, there is inadequate competition and very little grantee turnover. For example, all 52 grantees receiving employment and training grants in 2017 had also been awarded grants in the previous competition, even though their performance was mixed.

REDUCTION: OFFICE OF DISABILITY EMPLOYMENT POLICY
Department of Labor

The Budget proposes $27 million, returning the Office of Disability Employment Policy (ODEP) closer to its core mission of policy development, technical assistance, and dissemination of effective practices to increase the employment of people with disabilities. The 2019 Budget also proposes to continue the Retaining Employment and Talent after Injury/Illness Network (RETAIN) demonstration project to test effective interventions to promote greater labor force participation of people with disabilities.

Funding Summary
(In millions of dollars)

	2017 Enacted	2019 Request	2019 Change from 2017
Budget Authority...	38	27	-11

Justification

The Congress created ODEP in 2001 to bring a heightened focus on disability employment in the Federal Government through policy analysis, technical assistance, and development of best practices.

ODEP was tasked with implementing a sustained, coordinated, and aggressive employment strategy to eliminate job barriers for people with disabilities. However, ODEP has since expanded its responsibilities beyond its original mission to include numerous grant programs on a wide range of activities. This includes support services, such as ODEP's grants for technical assistance for accessible technology and career development in post-secondary education, that duplicate activities supported by the Departments of Education, Health and Human Services, and other agencies. The 2019 Budget would eliminate duplicative grant making activities and refocus the Office on developing, testing, and implementing disability employment policies to increase the recruitment, retention and advancement of people with disabilities.

The Budget also proposes to replace one of ODEP's major initiatives, the Disability Employment Initiative (DEI), that since 2010 has provided grants to State workforce agencies to improve American Job Center capacity to serve individuals with disabilities. The Federal Government already provides substantial funding to States for their workforce system, and States are required by law to provide reasonable accommodation to individuals with disabilities to ensure that they can participate. In addition, preliminary results suggest that DEI has shown weak impacts; an interim report showed no statistically significant difference between the treatment and control group in terms of wages or employment placement rates.[1]

The Budget proposes to redeploy DEI funding for a new demonstration project modeled on Washington State's successful Centers of Occupational Health and Education (COHE) program to improve labor force participation and attachment of individuals with temporary injuries and disabilities. The demonstration, which will be operated in partnership with the Social Security Administration, will test the effects of implementing key features of the COHE model in other States or municipalities and/or for a broader population beyond recipients of workers' compensation. Key features include care and service coordination, population screening and monitoring, increased access and targeted vocational rehabilitation and work supports, workplace accommodations, and technical assistance to healthcare providers and employers. Optional interventions that could be tested by grantees include additional income support in absence of other temporary disability supports, partial wage support to allow for part-time return-to-work, increased access to specific medical or holistic care, and employer incentives.

Past efforts provided enhanced incentives to pursue work for people with disabilities who spent years out of the labor force. In contrast, this early intervention return-to-work initiative is aimed at helping the individual worker maintain attachment to the labor force and self-sufficiency.

Citations

[1] Social Dynamics, LLC, and Mathematica Policy Research: *DEI Interim Synthesis Report For Year 4,* (August 2016).

ELIMINATION: OSHA TRAINING GRANTS
Department of Labor

The Budget proposes to eliminate the Occupational Safety and Health Administration's (OSHA) Susan Harwood training grants, which are unnecessary and unproven.

Funding Summary
(In millions of dollars)

	2017 Enacted	2019 Request	2019 Change from 2017
Budget Authority...	11	0	-11

Justification

OSHA's Harwood Training Grant program was established in 1978 to provide one- to five-year competitive grants to non-profit organizations to develop and conduct occupational safety and health training programs. OSHA has no evidence that the program is effective, and measures the program's performance in terms of the number of individuals trained. In addition, it is not clear that the training funded by these grants would not happen absent the Federal subsidy. The Budget proposes to provide resources for OSHA's compliance assistance activities, including free on-site safety and health consultations for small businesses; cooperative programs to help employers identify and address hazards; and assistance to help employers and workers improve the safety of their workplaces. The House Appropriations Committee marks zeroed out this program in 2016 and 2017, stating concerns that is was less effective than other forms of OSHA compliance assistance.

ELIMINATION: SENIOR COMMUNITY SERVICE EMPLOYMENT PROGRAM
Department of Labor

The Budget proposes to eliminate the Senior Community Service Employment Program (SCSEP). SCSEP is ineffective in achieving its goal of transitioning seniors into unsubsidized employment.

Funding Summary
(In millions of dollars)

	2017 Enacted	2019 Request	2019 Change from 2017
Budget Authority...	400	0	-400

Justification

SCSEP distributes grants to States and public and private non-profit organizations to provide part-time work experience in community service activities to unemployed low-income persons ages 55 and over.

While the program provides some income support to about 60,000 individuals each year, it fails to meet its other major statutory goals of fostering economic self-sufficiency and moving low-income seniors into unsubsidized employment. SCSEP has a goal of transitioning half of participants into unsubsidized employment within the first quarter after exiting the program, but has struggled to achieve even this modest goal, doing so in only one of the most recent seven program years.[1] Further, these placement rates exclude the nearly one half of program participants who do not complete the program and are excluded from the measure. With costs of more than $7,300 per participant, it is not a cost-effective mechanism to facilitate community service among older adults. The goal of supporting the self-sufficiency and employment to older workers can continue to be addressed through the Workforce Innovation and Opportunity Act (WIOA) programs.

Citations

[1] Department of Labor: *Senior Community Service Employment Program: Nationwide Quarterly Progress Reports*, 2010–2016, ETA 5140, www.doleta.gov/Seniors/html_docs/GranteePerf.cfm.

ELIMINATION: DEVELOPMENT ASSISTANCE
Department of State and U.S. Agency for International Development

The Budget proposes to refocus, reduce, and consolidate economic and development assistance across budget accounts, countries, and sectors in order to better prioritize core programs and approaches for implementing the National Security Strategy, support partner countries of greatest strategic importance, and ensure the effectiveness of U.S. taxpayer investments. The Budget proposes to eliminate the Development Assistance (DA) account and to fund selected programs previously covered by the account through the new consolidated Economic Support and Development Fund, enabling and reflecting a more balanced consideration of how these programs support U.S. national security and economic interests.

Funding Summary
(In millions of dollars)

	2017 Enacted	2019 Request	2019 Change from 2017
Budget Authority..	2,835	0	-2,835

Note: The FY 2017 Enacted level for the Development Assistance account in this table excludes $160 million for climate-change activities that is described in the Global Climate Change Initiative elimination. The total enacted level for Developmental Assistance is $2,995 million.

Justification

Consistent with the Administration's goals of streamlining foreign assistance and freeing up funding for strengthening the Nation's military and for pursuing critical priorities here at home, the Budget proposes to eliminate the DA account. Selected countries and programs previously covered by the DA account would be supported through the Economic Support and Development Fund (ESDF), allowing the Department of State (State) and U.S. Agency for International Development (USAID) to better assess, prioritize, and target development-related activities in the context of broader U.S. strategic objectives and partnerships around the world. Having one streamlined account for economic and development assistance would also increase State and USAID's flexibility to trade off needs on an even footing and address emerging challenges and opportunities within one account. This approach is parallel to the Budget's proposed treatment of other similar accounts, such as the Assistance for Europe, Eurasia and Central Asia (AEECA) account, in that it allows State and USAID to treat regions, sectors, and countries on an equivalent basis, avoiding the sometimes suboptimal allocations that result from directed funding.

Instead, in ESDF, the Budget proposes to refocus economic and development assistance on countries and sectors that would best protect the American people and the homeland; promote U.S. prosperity and economic opportunities for U.S. businesses; and advance American interests and values around the world. The Budget also recognizes that it's *how* the U.S. spends its foreign aid, and not *how much,* that is most important for advancing our goals and supporting our partners. It proposes to apply economic and development assistance in a more targeted and effective manner, where and how it's needed based on measures of development progress, to advance countries' self-reliance and ultimately end their reliance on external aid. The Budget proposes a new domestic resource mobilization initiative and a new, enhanced U.S. Development Finance Institution that will build the capacity and capability of developing countries and the private sector to drive sustainable change and economic growth, and thereby reduce the need for traditional development assistance, and reduce risks and costs to the American taxpayer. The Budget would also set the expectation that other donors would need to step up and do their fair share to support economic growth and development worldwide, and that aid programs must be coupled with strong accountability and improved processes to track data and apply evidence of what works to program design.

ELIMINATION: EARMARKED APPROPRIATIONS FOR NON-PROFIT ORGANIZATIONS
Department of State and U.S. Agency for International Development

The Budget continues to support the elimination of earmarked appropriations for the East-West Center and The Asia Foundation given these organizations serve niche missions that duplicate other Federal programs. Elimination of earmarked Federal funding will not terminate these organizations, due to their non-profit status, and they remain eligible and are encouraged to compete for Federal grant funding and may receive private sector contributions.

Funding Summary
(In millions of dollars)

	2017 Enacted	2019 Request	2019 Change from 2017
The Asia Foundation..	17	0	-17
East-West Center..	17	0	-17

Justification

The East-West Center (EWC) is a quasi-governmental organization established by the Congress in 1960, and The Asia Foundation (TAF) is a private, non-governmental organization founded in 1954. Even though these organizations remain authorized, it is highly unusual for private organizations to receive a direct appropriation with no direct leadership from the Executive Branch to provide oversight. The Administration continues to support ending dedicated funding for organizations that may effectively serve niche missions, but which are not critical to the conduct of U.S. foreign policy and which duplicate the efforts of other Federal programs or the non-profit and private sectors. By making this change, EWC and TAF will be incentivized to compete for Federal funding which will improve efficiency while minimizing the potential for duplication.

REDUCTION: EDUCATIONAL AND CULTURAL EXCHANGES
Department of State and U.S. Agency for International Development

The Budget proposes to significantly reduce Federal funding for the Department of State's Educational and Cultural Exchange Programs, including the Bureau of Educational and Cultural Affairs (ECA). Federal support for educational and cultural exchanges requested in the Budget would be focused on efficient and effective programs that help build networks of leaders abroad to promote a more free and prosperous world. Program resources for people-to-people exchanges would support strategic foreign policy objectives that benefit Americans.

Funding Summary
(In millions of dollars)

	2017 Enacted	2019 Request	2019 Change from 2017
Budget Authority..	634	159	-475

Justification

When originally authorized (Mutual Educational and Cultural Exchange Act of 1961), educational and cultural exchanges were an important means of exposing foreign citizens to U.S. culture, and U.S. citizens to foreign culture. The State Department currently manages over 85 separate academic, professional, and cultural exchange programs — double the number that existed in 2004. Having so many different exchange programs dilutes their overall impact and presents challenges to effective program management. Reducing the number of exchange programs to a core few would allow the State Department to focus its management and oversight resources on those programs that have demonstrated results. In addition, globalization has increased significantly since the start of people-to-people exchanges, students as well as other international visitors largely rely on personal and family[1] as primary sources of funding and support.

The fact that private-sector Exchange Visitor (J-1 Visa) Program (EVP) has grown in popularity, without requiring any Federal allocation or subsidy, demonstrates that there is widespread demand in the marketplace to support the cultural exchange opportunities. For example, in 2017, the private sector supported nearly five times the number of EVP participants[2] (estimated 300,000) as were supported through Federal funding of ECA's exchange programs[2] (estimated 60,000). While these programs were launched to support international travel when the vast majority of families and countries could not afford to send students and young leaders abroad, this is simply no longer the case. As a general matter, many professionals travel during U.S. funded exchange programs from highly industrialized economies in Western Europe and parts of Asia that should fund their own participant's travel costs. Reductions to ECA's budget would allow it to focus resources on programs that have the most potential for positive impacts, and to support participants in the most financial need (i.e. participants who would otherwise be unable to travel without U.S. Government support).

The United States is the top destination for university abroad, welcoming over one million students whose attendance contribute to the US economy[3] and help make America prosperous. As such, funding dollars would be prioritized for countries, partners, and activities that advance foreign policy objectives, continue to promote U.S. higher education abroad, and benefit Americans. The proposed funding level seeks to rebalance the use of Government resources for educational and cultural exchanges with the availability of private sector funding and partner governments. Program resources would be more narrowly targeted towards specific foreign policy priorities while avoiding duplication.

Citations

[1] Institute for International Education: *Research and Insights, Open Doors 2017 Fast Facts, (2017)*

[2] U.S. Department of State, Bureau of Educational and Cultural Affairs

[3] National Association of Foreign Student Advisers (NAFSA): *The United States of America Benefits from International Students, NAFSA's Economic Analysis for 2016-2017 Academic Year (2017)*

ELIMINATION: GLOBAL CLIMATE CHANGE INITIATIVE
Department of State and U.S. Agency for International Development

Consistent with the President's plan to withdraw from the Paris Agreement on climate change, the Budget proposes to eliminate the Global Climate Change Initiative (GCCI) and wind down funding for State Department and U.S. Agency for International Development (USAID) bilateral activities with partner countries that are specifically intended to address climate change. The last administration committed over $1.5 billion to the GCCI in its final year, 2016. By contrast, eliminating the GCCI would enable the State Department and USAID to focus taxpayer dollars on their core missions to protect the American people and preserve our way of life; promote U.S. prosperity; and advance American interests and values around the world.

Funding Summary
(In millions of dollars)

	2017 Enacted	2019 Request	2019 Change from 2017
Bilateral GCCI (Base Budget Authority)..	160	0	-160

Justification

The Paris Agreement, as it stands, does not equally share burdens and responsibilities among the nations of the world, and unfairly places the U.S. at a financial disadvantage. In the single year of 2016 funding, the previous administration provided over $1.5 billion to the GCCI, including $1 billion for the Green Climate Fund alone. Instead of using such funds to help other countries address climate change, even while many of them plan to increase their emissions, the U.S. should invest in our own economic growth. The Administration, working with the Congress, successfully zeroed out the Green Climate Fund in 2017 appropriations. The Budget proposes to fully eliminate the GCCI because we must focus on our own prosperity and the appropriate balance between economic growth and environmental leadership, in order to bring jobs, factories, and production back to the U.S.. We must put the energy and economic needs of American families and businesses first through a plan that ensures energy security and economic vitality for decades to come, including by promoting development of the Nation's vast energy resources. While the U.S. will continue to engage internationally to protect U.S. energy security and economic interests and to achieve a level playing field, the Budget proposes to wind down existing State Department and USAID bilateral programs intended primarily to help other countries mitigate the impacts of climate change. The Budget continues support for developing countries' efforts to improve affordable and reliable energy access; agricultural and economic resilience; and natural resource use and management, where mutually beneficial to our broader foreign policy, economic development, and national security objectives.

REDUCTION: INTERNATIONAL ORGANIZATION CONTRIBUTIONS
Department of State and U.S. Agency for International Development

The Budget proposes to end or reduce funding for international programs and organizations whose missions do not substantially advance U.S. foreign policy interests, or for which the funding burden is not fairly shared among members. Funding for these organizations is currently provided in two accounts: dues and other assessed support is through Contributions to International Organizations (CIO); and additional voluntary contributions are provided through International Organizations and Programs (IOP). No funding for the IOP account is requested in the Budget.

Funding Summary
(In millions of dollars)

	2017 Enacted	2019 Request	2019 Change from 2017
Base Budget Authority..	1,602	899	-703
Overseas Contingency Operations...	96	96	0
Total Budget Authority..	1,698	995	-703

Note: The amounts for 2017 Enacted in the table combine funding for the Contributions to International Organizations (CIO) account and the International Organizations and Programs (IOP) account.

Justification

The Budget requests $995 million for contributions to the United Nations (UN), technical agencies, and other international organizations, while signaling our continued pursuit of greater accountability and emphasizing shared responsibility among members. The United States is just one of 193 countries in the UN but pays for 22 percent of the regular budget, more than any other country, and more than the combined contributions of all four of the other permanent members with veto power in the UN Security Council. The Administration remains committed to the need for greater transparency and reform in international bodies and for other donors to invest more. In support of these goals, the Department of State will continue to review multilateral contributions to evaluate how each organization to which the United States belongs advances American interests. The Administration has begun to make progress on this effort and the Budget reflects a commitment to achieving better outcomes within multilateral organizations.

In December of 2017, the UN agreed on a budget for calendar years 2018-2019 that reflected a negotiated reduction by the U.S., with like-minded partners including the European Union and Japan, of over $285 million below the 2016-2017 final budget. In addition to these significant cost savings, the U.S. reduced the UN's bloated management and support functions, bolstered support for key U.S. priorities throughout the world, and instilled more discipline and accountability throughout the UN system. As stated by Ambassador Haley, "The inefficiency and overspending of the United Nations are well known. We will no longer let the generosity of the American people be taken advantage of or remain unchecked. This historic reduction in spending – in addition to many other moves toward a more efficient and accountable UN – is a big step in the right direction. While we are pleased with the results of this year's budget negotiations, you can be sure we'll continue to look at ways to increase the UN's efficiency while protecting our interests."

In reviewing U.S. membership in international organizations, the Department of State notified the United Nations Educational and Cultural Organization (UNESCO) last year of the U.S. decision to withdraw from the organization. This decision reflected U.S. concerns with the need for fundamental reform in the organization and continuing anti-Israel bias at UNESCO.

To the extent the U.S. decides to pursue continued funding for any of the organizations previously supported via IOP, the Budget assumes that it would do so in 2019 through the Economic Support and Development Fund and other foreign assistance accounts.

REDUCTION: OVERSEAS CONTINGENCY OPERATIONS
Department of State and U.S. Agency for International Development

Overseas Contingency Operations (OCO) funding has been used during the annual appropriations process as a means to evade the budget caps by supporting more and more long-term, ongoing activities with contingency funding that falls outside the statutory budget caps. The 2019 request renews the effort that was started in the 2018 Budget to begin phasing out OCO funding that is not for temporary and extraordinary contingency needs of the Department of State and U.S. Agency for International Development (State/USAID).

Funding Summary
(In millions of dollars)

	2017 Enacted	2019 Request	2019 Change from 2017
Overseas Contingency Operations..	20,785	12,017	-8,768

Note: The 2017 Enacted total includes $4,300 million enacted in the Further Continuing and Security Assistance Appropriations Act (Public Law 114-254) for counter-ISIS activities.

Justification

State/USAID was first appropriated OCO funding in 2012 to fund temporary and extraordinary needs related to the wars in Iraq and Afghanistan. Each year since, during the appropriations process, enduring State/USAID funding has been shifted from base to OCO to create a relief valve to free up funding for other non-defense discretionary (NDD) priorities, and relieve the cap pressures faced by all NDD agencies and programs. While some needs for State/USAID contingency funding have legitimately grown since 2012 (*e.g.*, the conflict in Syria), the use of OCO to fund enduring State/USAID activities has been greatly expanded beyond its original intent, to include critical activities that are neither temporary nor extraordinary, but are instead ongoing and anticipated.

The 2017 Enacted level for State/USAID OCO funding ballooned to the highest ever level of $20.8 billion, representing 37 percent of total Agency funding and allocated across 21 accounts and over 50 countries for a broad range of ongoing activities. This total included $16.5 billion in regular appropriations and an additional $4.3 billion provided in the Further Continuing and Security Assistance Appropriations Act (SAAA) for counter-ISIS activities. By comparison, in the 2012 Request, the OCO level for State/USAID represented just 16 percent of the Agency budget and was allocated for extraordinary program levels in just three countries — Iraq, Afghanistan, and Pakistan — across just six accounts.

The 2019 Budget repeats the proposal from the 2018 Budget to begin reining in the expansion of State/USAID OCO funding and shifting funding for ongoing activities, such as embassy construction, back into the base.

ELIMINATION: P.L. 480 TITLE II FOOD AID
Department of State and U.S. Agency for International Development

The Budget proposes to eliminate the P.L. 480 Title II food aid program (Title II) in order to focus on the highest priority, most efficient and effective foreign assistance, and eliminate inefficient, slow, and high-cost programs. The foreign assistance request retains sufficient funding for emergency food assistance in the International Disaster Assistance (IDA) account, which already provides food aid through the most effective means for each crisis and provides U.S. food commodities where they are the most appropriate emergency response.

Funding Summary
(In millions of dollars)

	2017 Enacted	2019 Request	2019 Change from 2017
Budget Authority..	1,600	0	-1,600

Justification

The Title II program provides emergency and development food aid, mainly through the purchase and shipment of U.S. commodities. The Budget focuses humanitarian and development assistance on the highest priorities and proposes to eliminate duplicative and inefficient programs. Providing emergency food aid through IDA has been shown to allow more appropriate and on average more cost effective assistance than Title II food aid. Unlike Title II, IDA is able to adjust to conflict and other situations (such as the Syria crisis) where affected people may be displaced multiple times. Procuring food near crises can save up to two months or more on delivery time and can significantly reduce the costs of food aid. In addition, such purchases and other tools such as cash vouchers, where appropriate, also help support local economies shaken by humanitarian crises, which can lower overall needs. Given limited resources, it is important to focus funding on the most efficient assistance mechanisms. In this case, IDA allows the choice of the right tool at the right time and maximizes the reach of U.S. assistance.

Disproportionate share of global food aid—The United States is the largest provider of emergency food aid, typically accounting for a third or more of all contributions. As the United States refocuses assistance to the highest priority areas, the Budget calls upon other donors to do their fair share.

Slower and more costly—Title II takes an average of four to six months to deliver food aid, which means that food may need to be moved before it is certain that it is needed (such as anticipating whether and how severe a drought may be) or shipments may arrive too late. Using IDA can significantly shorten the delivery time. In some disasters, IDA has allowed food to arrive within days, not months. While in certain cases Title II can be prepositioned to save some time, the additional storage, handling, and delivery costs mean that U.S. taxpayers are paying even more compared to the costs of IDA.

Less efficient than other foreign assistance—Title II requires that at least 20 percent of annual appropriations (with a minimum of $350 million per year) must be used for development food aid programs. At least 15 percent of the U.S. commodities for these programs must be sold abroad, typically at an average loss of 25 percent or more of the cost. The proceeds of these sales, referred to as monetization, are used to fund development programs, and the loss on these sales is paid for by U.S. taxpayers. Eliminating these programs would align with the approach taken toward other foreign assistance programs, ensuring that funding can be focused on the highest priorities, on efficiency, and on effectiveness. The U.S. Agency for International Development would continue to fund longer-term food security and nutrition programs through the Economic Support and Development Fund and the Global Health Program.

REDUCTION: PEACEKEEPING
Department of State and U.S. Agency for International Development

The Budget would support a United States contribution at or below the statutory cap of 25 percent for United Nations (UN) peacekeeping missions in the Contributions to International Peacekeeping Activities (CIPA) account. The U.S. would continue to work with the UN to constrain peacekeeping costs, eliminate missions as conditions warrant, and achieve greater operational and management efficiencies. The Budget proposes to eliminate funding for duplicative capacity building programs in the Peacekeeping Operations (PKO) account.

Funding Summary
(In millions of dollars)

	2017 Enacted	2019 Request	2019 Change from 2017
Base Budget Authority..	688	356	-332
Overseas Contingency Operations...	1,879	1,132	-747
Total Budget Authority..	2,567	1,488	-1,079

Note: The amounts in the table combine funding for the Contributions to International Peacekeeping (CIPA) account and Peacekeeping Operations (PKO) account.

Justification

With over 100,000 personnel and an annual budget of over $7 billion, UN peacekeeping is a powerful tool to address challenges to international peace and security. However, peacekeeping missions alone cannot achieve lasting peace and must be part of a larger strategic context that includes political solutions to these protracted conflicts. Furthermore, reform is needed to create not only more efficient and accountable peacekeeping operations but to ensure that each mission's mandate reflects the realities on the ground and is supported by the necessary political will and structures to achieve its objectives. Over the last year, the U.S. has articulated the need for reform and core principles that guide our assessment of mission effectiveness and mandates.

The Budget request of $1.2 billion for U.S. contributions to UN peacekeeping activities supports a United States contribution at or below the statutory cap of 25 percent for UN peacekeeping missions. At an assessed rate of 28.47 percent, the United States pays more than its fair share of the cost, particularly when the other four permanent UN Security Council members with veto power are assessed between four and ten percent. The Budget continues to reinforce the expectation that the UN would reduce costs by reevaluating the design and implementation of peacekeeping missions and sharing the funding burden more fairly among members. While the recent negotiations for the current UN peacekeeping budget yielded over half a billion dollars in savings, more work needs to be done. The U.S. will continue to work with the Secretary General and members of the Security Council to increase mission effectiveness and reduce the overall peacekeeping budget.

The Budget request of $291 million for PKO would support multilateral peacekeeping and regional stability operations that are not funded by the UN, help build operational readiness and sustainment capabilities for partner countries deploying to peace operations, and build the military capacity of regional partners to counter terrorism. The Administration continues to propose the elimination of programs in the account that are duplicative of ongoing bilateral and global capacity building programs.

REDUCTION: CAPITAL INVESTMENT GRANTS (NEW STARTS)
Department of Transportation

The Budget proposes to limit funding for the Federal Transit Administration's Capital Investment Grants program to projects with existing full funding grant agreements only. Under the infrastructure initiative, if regions raise their own dedicated revenues for infrastructure, the Administration would reward them with competitive grants and other incentives, and those regions can decide to use those funds for transit investment. Similarly, while the Budget proposes to wind down the Capital Investment Grants program, Federal innovative financing tools would remain available to advance transit projects.

Funding Summary
(In millions of dollars)

	2017 Enacted	2019 Request	2019 Change from 2017
Budget Authority..	2,413	1,000	-1,413

Justification

The Budget proposes reduced funding for this program, which provides Federal funding for local transit projects that should be funded by States and localities that benefit from their use. The President's Infrastructure Initiative is designed to incentivize States and localities to raise new revenue and funding dedicated for infrastructure investment, via competitive Federal grant awards and other incentives. Those new State and local funds would be available to transportation projects prioritized by those communities, which are better equipped to understand their infrastructure needs. The Federal Government would continue to be a partner in advancing large, regionally- or nationally-significant projects via expanded Federal credit support.

REDUCTION: ESSENTIAL AIR SERVICE
Department of Transportation

The Budget proposes to reform the Essential Air Service (EAS) by reducing discretionary funding and focusing on the remote airports that are most in need of subsidized commercial air service. The proposal includes a mix of reforms, including limits on per-passenger subsidies and higher average daily enplanements.

Funding Summary
(In millions of dollars)

	2017 Enacted	2019 Request	2019 Change from 2017
Budget Authority..	150	93	-57

Justification

EAS was designed as a temporary program nearly 40 years ago to mitigate potential impacts from airline deregulation, and many EAS flights are not full and have extraordinarily high per-passenger subsidy costs. The average 2016 per-passenger subsidy for EAS communities in the Continental United States was $238, with a high of $778. Previous piecemeal efforts to reform the EAS program have failed. In constant 2016 dollars, EAS spending has increased 600 percent since 1996 and 132 percent since 2008. The average cost per community in the continental United States in 2016 was $2.5 million. Several EAS communities are close to other airports and have less than 10 average daily enplanements. Further, many communities have repeatedly received waivers if they did not meet the enplanement and subsidy cap requirements.

The Administration believes it is essential to comprehensively reform the EAS program, to finally bring spiraling costs under control, while ensuring that truly remote communities receive air service. The Budget includes a legislative reform proposal to ensure that Federal funds are efficiently targeted at the communities most in need. These reforms limit EAS eligibility to communities located more than 50 driving miles from a small hub, 75 miles from a medium hub, and 100 miles from a large hub. This recognizes the changing landscape since 1978 and the increased access to air service. The reforms would also increase the subsidy cap from $200 to $250 per passenger for communities located within 210 miles from a large or medium hub airport and eliminates the waiver for this requirement. Further, the reforms would place limits on the waiver authority for the 10-enplanement requirement.

REDUCTION: GRANTS TO AMTRAK
Department of Transportation

The Budget proposes a number of reforms to rationalize Amtrak's long distance trains, which transport a relatively small number of passengers but generate the vast majority of Amtrak's operating losses. The Budget proposes that States served by long distance trains begin to share in the operating costs with the Federal government. This proposal is one reform initiative out of a set of efforts the Administration will be exploring with stakeholders to reduce long distance operating losses and improve transportation options for the public. In line with overarching reforms to Amtrak, the Budget proposes funding for Amtrak's Northeast Corridor activities at a level that supports capital investments, but encourages Amtrak to increase efficiencies across all asset lines.

Funding Summary
(In millions of dollars)

	2017 Enacted	2019 Request	2019 Change from 2017
Budget Authority...	1,495	738	-757

Justification

Amtrak's Long Distance routes suffer from poor on-time performance; account for only 4.7 million of Amtrak's nearly 32 million annual passengers; and incur annual operating losses of more than $500 million. In particular, in 2017 the Sunset Limited Long Distance Route served 99,000 passengers, but generated a $38.4 million operating loss, resulting in a $351 Federal subsidy per passenger. Other Long Distance Routes, including the Southwest Chief, California Zephyr, and Empire Builder, required a subsidy of $118-$149 per passenger.

The approach to fund and operate the Long Distance network in its current iteration is not effective nor efficient. The Budget proposes reforms to rationalize the system, including implementing State contributions equal to the Federal Government for operational costs of Long Distance routes that serve their communities. The Budget proposes that States will begin to split the operating subsidy costs of Long Distance routes with the Federal Government. This proposal for greater State contributions aligns with the President's Infrastructure Initiative to encourage greater State and locality investment in infrastructure projects.

However, State contributions to Long Distance Routes is only one tool in the menu of options the Administration would explore with stakeholders to reduce Federal subsidies in the Long Distance network. The Administration believes Amtrak should utilize existing capabilities to reduce Long Distance costs, such as eliminating redundant routes and allowing ticketing for intra-NEC trips for Long Distance routes that operate over the NEC. Any Federal subsidies currently allocated to premium/first-class services provided by Amtrak – including sleeping cars, dining cars, and checked baggage – would also begin to be phased out and encouraged to be contracted out to private operators, or otherwise break even or eliminate these services.

The Budget proposes funding to the critical NEC at a level that supports capital investments, but encourages Amtrak to increase efficiencies across all asset lines.

ELIMINATION: NATIONAL INFRASTRUCTURE INVESTMENTS (TIGER)
Department of Transportation

The Budget proposes to eliminate funding for the unauthorized TIGER discretionary grant program, which awards grants to projects that may have only localized benefits and are generally eligible for funding under other surface transportation formula grant and loan programs.

Funding Summary
(In millions of dollars)

	2017 Enacted	2019 Request	2019 Change from 2017
Budget Authority..	500	0	-500

Justification

This program began as part of the 2009 stimulus bill and has not been authorized under the last two multi-year surface transportation authorization acts. It provides Federal funding for projects with localized benefits, and often these projects do not rise to the level of national or regional significance. For example, TIGER grants have been used for sidewalks, street furniture, tree planting, shared use paths, and on-street parking spaces. Further, this program is similar to the Department of Transportation's Nationally Significant Freight and Highway Projects grant program, authorized by the FAST Act of 2015, which supports larger highway and multimodal freight projects with demonstrable national or regional benefits. The Nationally Significant Freight and Highway Projects grant program is authorized at an annual average of $900 million through 2020. In addition, projects eligible for TIGER grants generally are eligible for other surface transportation grants and loan programs.

REDUCTION: RAILROAD SAFETY USER FEE
Department of Transportation

Railroads benefit directly and indirectly from the Federal Government's efforts to ensure high safety standards through the Federal Railroad Administration's rail safety inspectors and activities, and it is appropriate for railroads, like other regulated industries, to partially fund Federal safety efforts.

Funding Summary
(In millions of dollars)

	2017 Enacted	2019 Request	2019 Change from 2017
Fees..	0	-50	-50

Justification

The Budget proposes to reinstate the Railroad Safety User Fee, which was originally authorized by the Congress in 1990 and implemented by the Federal Railroad Administration between 1991 and 1995. However, the Congress repealed the provision for this fee in September 1995. Reinstatement of this user fee would support the Federal Government's cost for rail safety inspectors and rail safety activities, and would help balance costs funded by taxpayers and those borne by the railroad operators that benefit directly and indirectly from the program. This model is not unique in the Department of Transportation; for instance, the Pipeline and Hazardous Materials Safety Administration partially offsets its safety regulation activities with fees on oil and gas pipeline operators.

REDUCTION: COMMUNITY DEVELOPMENT FINANCIAL INSTITUTIONS FUND
Department of the Treasury

The Budget proposes to eliminate funding for the Community Development Financial Institutions (CDFI) Fund's grant programs, but requests $14 million for oversight of existing commitments and administration of the CDFI Fund's other programs. The CDFI industry has matured, and these institutions should have access to private capital needed to build capacity, extend credit, and provide financial services to the communities they serve.

Funding Summary
(In millions of dollars)

	2017 Enacted	2019 Request	2019 Change from 2017
CDFI Fund Grants..	222	0	-222
CDFI Fund Administration...	26	14	-12
Total Budget Authority...	248	14	-234

Justification

Created in 1994, but currently unauthorized, the CDFI Fund provides grants, loans, and tax credits to a national network of CDFIs to expand the availability of credit, investment capital, and financial services for underserved people and communities. Today, there are over 1,100 Treasury-certified CDFIs — including loan funds, community development banks, credit unions, and venture capital funds — active in all 50 States and the District of Columbia. The Budget proposes to eliminate funding for the Fund's four discretionary grant and direct loan programs targeted at this now mature industry. However, it would maintain funding for administrative expenses to support ongoing CDFI Fund program activities, including the New Markets Tax Credit program, and would extend the CDFI Bond Guarantee Program, which offers CDFIs low-cost, long-term financing at no cost to taxpayers, as the program requires no credit subsidy.

ELIMINATION: MULTILATERAL AGRICULTURAL DEVELOPMENT PROGRAMS
Department of the Treasury

The Budget does not propose funding for two multilateral programs funded in 2017: the Global Agriculture and Food Security Program (GAFSP), and the International Fund for Agricultural Development (IFAD), both of which support agricultural development in poor countries. Agricultural development funding by the multilateral development banks (MDBs) dwarfs GAFSP and IFAD, while the U.S. Agency for International Development (USAID) bilateral food security programs focus related funding in areas of particular interest to the United States.

Funding Summary
(In millions of dollars)

	2017 Enacted	2019 Request	2019 Change from 2017
GAFSP	23	0	-23
IFAD	30	0	-30

Justification

GAFSP is a multi-donor trust fund that supports agricultural investment plans of poor countries, while IFAD is a UN specialized agency that provides agricultural programs focused mainly on remote rural areas of poor countries seeking a new replenishment of donor funds in 2019.

With the completion of funding for the last IFAD replenishment (IFAD-10) in 2018, the U.S. will further focus its food security funding on USAID bilateral programs for agricultural development and food security. USAID programs are specifically designed to have significant impacts on malnutrition and poverty, include stringent outcome measures of performance, and are aligned with U.S. strategic priorities. USAID programs also have a major focus on increasing resilience of vulnerable populations and addressing the root causes of recurrent food crises in countries that receive significant U.S. humanitarian assistance.

In addition to bilateral funding, the United States Government and other donors support the same type of agricultural investments in poor countries through other mechanisms, and in particular through MDBs. MDB annual funding for agricultural development is several billion dollars per year. To the extent that there are lessons learned from IFAD and GAFSP, MDBs can be encouraged to employ them in their program selection and implementation.

For GAFSP, the 2012 pledge period is over. The United States contributed $475 million towards the initial GAFSP pledge in 2009. In 2012, the U.S. pledged to contribute $1 for every $2 dollars in new contributions from other donors over the announced period of the pledge, up to a maximum of $475 million. That period has ended, and the United States has sufficient prior-year funding to fulfill the pledge to match other donors' contributions.

Other donors' support of GAFSP has been limited. While other donors may continue to support GAFSP, their support for the 2012 pledge has been moderate at best. From 2012 to 2017, other donors' actual contributions totaled $356 million, and the United States contributed $178 million in matching funds. Only 10 donors provided funding for GAFSP since its inception, contributing less than $1.7 billion in total, with the United States counting for 42 percent of the initial pledge and $653 million, or 40 percent, of all contributions since 2009.

REDUCTION: SPECIAL INSPECTOR GENERAL FOR THE TROUBLED ASSET RELIEF PROGRAM

Department of the Treasury

The Budget reduces funding for the Special Inspector General for the Troubled Asset Relief Program (SIGTARP) commensurate with the wind-down of TARP programs.

Funding Summary
(In millions of dollars)

	2017 Enacted	2019 Request	2019 Change from 2017
Budget Authority...	41	18	-23

Justification

The Emergency Economic Stabilization Act of 2008 (P.L. 110-343) created SIGTARP and tasked the office with conducting, supervising, and coordinating audits and investigations of the purchase, management, and sale of assets by the Secretary of the Treasury under TARP. The Congress aligned the sunset of SIGTARP with the length of time that TARP funds or commitments are outstanding. Treasury estimates all programs will substantially close by 2023, at which time the last payments under the Home Affordable Modification Program are expected to occur.

Funding for SIGTARP is reduced, reflecting that less than one percent of Treasury's TARP investments remain outstanding, over 90 percent of Housing Finance Agency Hardest Hit Funds have been disbursed, and the application periods for the Federal Housing Administration Refinance program and Making Home Affordable initiative have ended. SIGTARP will retain access to mandatory funding provided in previous years that will help the office manage an orderly wind-down of its operations.

REDUCTION: CATEGORICAL GRANTS
Environmental Protection Agency

The Environmental Protection Agency (EPA) provides categorical grants to help fund State environmental program offices and activities. Many States have been delegated authority to implement and enforce Federal environmental laws including the Clean Air Act, Clean Water Act, and Safe Drinking Water Act. The Budget proposes to reduce many of these grants and eliminate others to better focus and prioritize environmental activities on core functions required by Federal environmental laws. The Budget also proposes a new categorical grant to provide States additional flexibility in how they meet their mandatory Federal statutory environmental requirements.

Funding Summary
(In millions of dollars)

	2017 Enacted	2019 Request	2019 Change from 2017
Budget Authority..	1,066	597	-469

Justification

EPA categorical grant funding is intended to help States meet Federal environmental law requirements and standards. The Budget proposes to eliminate or substantially reduce Federal investment in State environmental activities that go beyond EPA's statutory requirements. States could adjust to reduced funding levels by reducing or eliminating additional activities not required under Federal law, prioritizing programs, and seeking other funding sources including fees. The Budget also proposes a new categorical grant (Multipurpose Grants) to respond to State requests for additional flexibility in how they can spend categorical grants. These Multipurpose Grants would be available for any delegated mandatory statutory duty to help avoid the creation of unfunded mandates.

REDUCTION: ENERGY STAR AND VOLUNTARY CLIMATE PROGRAMS
Environmental Protection Agency

The Budget includes a proposal to authorize the Environmental Protection Agency (EPA) to administer the ENERGY STAR program through the collection of user fees. The Budget also proposes to eliminate funding for several voluntary partnership programs related to energy and climate change. These programs are not essential to EPA's core mission and can be implemented by the private sector.

Funding Summary
(In millions of dollars)

	2017 Enacted	2019 Request	2019 Change from 2017
Budget Authority...	66	0	-66

Justification

The Administration is committed to returning EPA to its core work. There is no need for EPA to administer voluntary partnership and certification programs with taxpayer dollars, given the popularity and significant private benefits these programs provide to industry partners and consumers. Similar voluntary programs have been, and continue to be, successfully administered by non-governmental entities like industry associations and consumer groups.

By administering the ENERGY STAR program through the collection of user fees, EPA would continue to provide a trusted resource for consumers and businesses who want to purchase products that save them money and help protect the environment. Product manufacturers who seek to label their products under the program would pay a modest fee that would support EPA's work to set voluntary energy efficiency standards and to process applications. Fee collections would begin after EPA undertakes a rulemaking process to determine which products would be covered by fees, the level of fees, and how to ensure that a fee system would not discourage manufacturers from participating in the program or result in a loss of environmental benefits.

REDUCTION: RESEARCH AND DEVELOPMENT
Environmental Protection Agency

The Budget proposes to reconfigure and restructure the Environmental Protection Agency's (EPA) activities in research and development to focus on research objectives that support statutory requirements. Extramural Science to Achieve Results (STAR) grants would not receive funding.

Funding Summary
(In millions of dollars)

	2017 Enacted	2019 Request	2019 Change from 2017
Budget Authority..	475	246	-229

Justification

As EPA shifts its programmatic resources to focus on core Agency responsibilities, the scientific research and development activities would also be reconfigured and restructured. At the proposed funding levels for the Office of Research and Development, the Agency would prioritize intramural research activities that are either related to statutory requirements or that support basic and early stage research and development activities in the environmental and human health sciences. EPA will continue to perform important environmental research to develop scientific and technological solutions that will improve air and water quality, such as developing methods to detect potentially harmful levels of chemicals like per- and polyfluoroalkyl substances (PFAS) in drinking and wastewaters. Additionally, EPA will carry out lead exposure modeling to help protect the health of vulnerable populations (including children) and will develop risk assessments to inform EPA decisions at Superfund, brownfield, and hazardous waste sites.

REDUCTION: SUPERFUND
Environmental Protection Agency

The Budget proposes to reduce funding for the Environmental Protection Agency's (EPA) Hazardous Substance Superfund Account, accounting for difficult decisions in the tight fiscal environment. The Budget would support EPA's efforts to rein in administrative costs, promote efficiencies, and encourage private investment in cleanup activities. The Budget would further support EPA's optimization of existing settlement funds for sites where those funds exist and strategies to remove some of the barriers that have delayed the program's ability to return sites to the community.

Funding Summary
(In millions of dollars)

	2017 Enacted	2019 Request	2019 Change from 2017
Budget Authority..	1,089	762	-327

Justification

The Hazardous Substance Superfund Account funds EPA's efforts to address the emergency release of hazardous substances and the long-term cleanup of hazardous waste sites. EPA relies on a combination of appropriated funds and settlements with responsible parties to perform its duties. There are over 1,300 active sites on the National Priorities List (NPL) of the most hazardous sites in the Nation, many of which have been on the NPL for decades. While a good portion of these sites include complex groundwater, soil, and sediment contamination, some are viewed as languishing under red tape and increasing indirect costs rates. The EPA Administrator tasked a Superfund Task Force with developing recommendations for reinvigorating the program and completing cleanups so that sites can be returned to the communities. The Task Force offered 42 recommendations, addressing all stages of the program, including ideas for encouraging additional private investment. While this Budget recognizes fiscal constraints and proposes to reduce appropriated dollars, it would allow EPA to pursue the paths recommended by the Task Force; optimize the use of settlement funds for sites where those funds exist; encourage further private investment; and foster design solutions to overcome barriers to site reuse.

Citations

[1] U.S. Environmental Protection Agency: *Superfund Task Force Recommendations,* https://www.epa.gov/sites/production/files/2017-07/documents/superfund_task_force_report.pdf, (July 2017).

ELIMINATION: FIVE EARTH SCIENCE MISSIONS
National Aeronautics and Space Administration

The Budget proposes to terminate five Earth Science missions: Radiation Budget Instrument (RBI); Plankton; Aerosol; Cloud; ocean Ecosystem (PACE); Orbiting Carbon Observatory-3 (OCO-3); Deep Space Climate Observatory (DSCOVR) Earth-viewing instruments; and Climate Absolute Radiance and Refractivity Observatory (CLARREO) Pathfinder. The missions would be terminated and National Aeronautics and Space Administration (NASA) funding would be prioritized toward supporting an innovative and sustainable program of exploration with commercial and international partners.

Funding Summary
(In millions of dollars)

	2017 Enacted	2019 Request	2019 Change from 2017
Budget Authority..	133	0	-133

Justification

The missions proposed for termination are lower-priority science missions that cannot be accommodated under constrained budgets. The proposed termination of these five missions realigns the NASA Earth science portfolio to focus on the highest-priority missions for the science and applications communities within a balanced, comprehensive Earth science program.

The RBI would have flown on a future weather satellite to make measurements of the Earth's reflected sunlight and emitted thermal radiation. Similar instruments flying now, including on the recently launched NOAA-20 satellite, would continue to provide continuity for the data record. In January 2018 the Science Mission Directorate conducted a detailed review of the RBI project and recommended cancelling the project due to cost growth and technical challenges.

Measurements similar to those that would have been taken by the PACE and OCO-3 missions are or would be acquired by other satellites. Under this proposal, NASA would cease funding data processing for the DSCOVR Earth-viewing instruments, which provide images of the sunlit side of the Earth and measure the energy reflected and emitted from it. These instruments do not contribute to the core DSCOVR mission of providing measurements for space weather.

The CLARREO Pathfinder mission would have demonstrated measurement technologies for a larger, more expensive, potential future mission focused on improving detection of climate trends. Other missions funded by NASA are maintaining measurements needed for climate data records. The CLARREO Pathfinder mission is in the earliest stages of implementation and is proposed for elimination to achieve cost savings.

ELIMINATION: OFFICE OF EDUCATION
National Aeronautics and Space Administration

The Budget proposes to terminate the National Aeronautics and Space Administration's (NASA) Office of Education, and prioritize NASA funding toward supporting an innovative and sustainable program of exploration with commercial and international partners. The Office of Education provides grants to colleges and universities as well as informal education institutions such as museums and science centers.

Funding Summary
(In millions of dollars)

	2017 Enacted	2019 Request	2019 Change from 2017
Budget Authority...	100	0	-100

Justification

The Budget proposes the termination of the Office of Education, redirecting those funds to NASA's core mission of exploration. The Budget would support the Administration's new space exploration policy by redirecting funding to innovative new programs that support the new policy. Additionally, while output data (e.g., number of people funded, or number of events supported) has been tracked, outcome-related data demonstrating program effectiveness has been insufficient to assess the impact of the overall Office of Education portfolio.

NASA would continue to support other education activities, such as fellowships and the Science Activation Program within the Science Mission Directorate that are funded outside the Office of Education.

ELIMINATION: WFIRST SPACE TELESCOPE
National Aeronautics and Space Administration

The Budget proposes to terminate the Wide Field Infrared Survey Telescope (WFIRST), given higher priorities within the National Aeronautics and Space Administration (NASA) and the increasing cost of this telescope.

Funding Summary
(In millions of dollars)

	2017 Enacted	2019 Request	2019 Change from 2017
Budget Authority..	105	0	-105

Justification

Development of the WFIRST space telescope would have required a significant funding increase in 2019 and future years, with a total cost of more than $3 billion. Additionally, a recent independent review concluded that WFIRST was not executable within its previous budget. Given competing priorities at NASA, and budget constraints, developing another large space telescope immediately after completing the $8.8 billion James Webb Space Telescope is not a priority for the Administration. The Budget proposes to terminate WFIRST and redirect existing funds to other priorities of the science community, including completed astrophysics missions and research.

ELIMINATION: CHEMICAL SAFETY BOARD
Other Independent Agencies

The U.S. Chemical Safety and Hazard Investigation Board (CSB) is proposed for elimination, consistent with the Administration's efforts to eliminate agencies and programs that are largely duplicative of efforts carried out by other agencies.

Funding Summary
(In millions of dollars)

	2017 Enacted	2019 Request	2019 Change from 2017
Budget Authority...	11	9	-2

Justification

CSB is an independent agency authorized by the Clean Air Act Amendments of 1990, whose mission is to investigate accidents at chemical facilities to determine the conditions or circumstances that led to the accident. The Congress intended CSB to be an investigative arm that is wholly independent of the rulemaking, inspection, and enforcement authorities of its partner agencies in making recommendations to prevent similar accidents from occurring in the future. While CSB has done some useful work on its investigations, its overlap with other agency investigative authorities has often generated friction. The previous management sought to focus CSB's recommendations on the need for greater regulation of industry, which frustrated both regulators and industry. The pressure to tie investigations to management priorities culminated in whistleblower complaints that led to critical reports issued in 2014 by both the Environmental Protection Agency Office of the Inspector General and the U.S. House of Representatives Oversight and Government Reform Committee. CSB's new leadership is making progress on rectifying the previous management challenges, but due to the relative duplicative nature of its work, and the Administration's focus on streamlining functions across the Federal Government, the Budget continues to recommend eliminating the Agency.

ELIMINATION: CORPORATION FOR NATIONAL AND COMMUNITY SERVICE
Other Independent Agencies

The Budget proposes to eliminate the Corporation for National and Community Service (CNCS) and provide funding for the orderly shutdown of the Agency. Funding community service and subsidizing the operation of nonprofit organizations is outside the role of the Federal Government. To the extent these activities have value, they should be supported by the nonprofit and private sectors and not with Federal subsidies provided through the complex Federal grant structure run by CNCS.

Funding Summary
(In millions of dollars)

	2017 Enacted	2019 Request	2019 Change from 2017
Budget Authority..	1,030	123	-907

Justification

CNCS is a grant-making agency that funds service opportunities, promotes volunteering, and helps nonprofit organizations engage volunteers. Members funded through CNCS grants typically receive a living allowance and education award of over $5,000 for their service. While some of the programs supported by CNCS grants have demonstrated effectiveness, and CNCS has made progress in evaluating its programs, some of the Agency's programs struggle to measure and demonstrate their impact. In addition, the Agency has struggled to effectively implement complex program requirements and has faced significant management challenges.

Funding community service and subsidizing the operation of non-profit organizations is outside the proper role of the Federal Government. Over 60 million Americans perform volunteer activities in their communities each year, absent subsidies from the Federal Government, and would likely continue to do so after CNCS is eliminated.[1] Programs currently funded by CNCS that demonstrate value should be able to compete successfully for funding from individual donors and the nonprofit and private sectors.

Citations

[1] U.S. Department of Labor, Bureau of Labor Statistics: *Volunteering in the United States – 2015*, USDL-16-0363, (February 2016).

ELIMINATION: CORPORATION FOR PUBLIC BROADCASTING
Other Independent Agencies

The Budget proposes to eliminate Federal funding for the Corporation for Public Broadcasting (CPB) over a two year period. CPB grants represent a small share of the total funding for the Public Broadcasting Service (PBS) and National Public Radio (NPR), which primarily rely on private donations to fund their operations. To conduct an orderly transition away from Federal funding, the Budget requests $15.5 million in 2019 and $15 million in 2020, which would include funding for personnel costs of $16.2 million; rental costs of $8.9 million; and other costs totaling $5.4 million.

Funding Summary
(In millions of dollars)

	2017 Enacted	2019 Request	2019 Change from 2017
Budget Authority...	495	15	-480

Justification

CPB provides grants to qualified public television and radio stations to be used at their discretion for purposes related to program production or acquisition, as well as for general operations. CPB also supports the production and acquisition of radio and television programs for national distribution. CPB funding comprises about 15 percent of the total amount spent on public broadcasting, with the remainder coming from non-Federal sources, with many large stations raising an even greater share. This private fundraising has proven durable, negating the need for continued Federal subsidies. Services such as PBS and NPR, which receive funding from CPB, could make up the shortfall by increasing revenues from corporate sponsors, foundations, and members. In addition, alternatives to PBS and NPR programming have grown substantially since CPB was first established in 1967, greatly reducing the need for publicly funded programming options.

ELIMINATION: D.C. TUITION ASSISTANCE GRANTS
Other Independent Agencies

The Budget proposes to eliminate the unauthorized Federal Payment for Resident Tuition Support (D.C. Tuition Assistance Grants). D.C. residents may avail themselves of many other Federal programs available to all Americans.

Funding Summary
(In millions of dollars)

	2017 Enacted	2019 Request	2019 Change from 2017
Budget Authority..	40	0	-40

Justification

The D.C. College Access Act of 1999 was last reauthorized in 2008, and has been unauthorized since 2012. The Budget proposes to eliminate the Federal Payments supporting Tuition Assistance Grants. While this program has helped many D.C. residents afford college, the financial position of the D.C. government has significantly improved since 1999 providing D.C. with flexibility to allocate local funds to support its residents. There are many Federal programs available to all Americans that help ensure continued college access.

ELIMINATION: INSTITUTE OF MUSEUM AND LIBRARY SERVICES
Other Independent Agencies

The Budget proposes to eliminate the Institute of Museum and Library Services (IMLS), which provides funding to museums and libraries across the country through formula and competitive grant awards. IMLS's funding supplements local, State, and private funds, which provide the vast majority of funding to museums and libraries.

Funding Summary
(In millions of dollars)

	2017 Enacted	2019 Request	2019 Change from 2017
Budget Authority...	231	23	-208

Justification

IMLS provides funding to museums and libraries across the country through formula and competitive grant awards. IMLS provides $156 million in formula funds to State Library Administrative Agencies, and administers several smaller competitive grant programs for libraries and museums that fund activities such as scholarships for librarian training and digital resources to support educational, employment, and other training opportunities. IMLS's funding supplements local, State, and private funds, which provide the vast majority of funding to museums and libraries. Furthermore, given that IMLS primarily supports discrete, short-term projects as opposed to operation-sustaining funds, it is unlikely the elimination of IMLS would result in the closure of a significant number of libraries and museums.

ELIMINATION: INTERNATIONAL DEVELOPMENT FOUNDATIONS
Other Independent Agencies

The Budget proposes to consolidate small grants functions and assistance aimed at reaching poor and remote communities that is currently carried out by the African Development Foundation (ADF) and the Inter-American Foundation (IAF) into the U.S. Agency for International Development (USAID) in order to streamline functions across Government. The Budget proposes funding for one-time close-out costs for ADF and IAF, while also requesting new funding for grantmaking and select personnel though USAID (not included in the Funding Summary below).

Funding Summary
(In millions of dollars)

	2017 Enacted	2019 Request	2019 Change from 2017
African Development Foundation..	30	5	-25
Inter-American Foundation..	22	3	-19

Justification

ADF and IAF were first authorized over 30 years ago, but have both operated without an authorization since 1987. In light of limited U.S. foreign assistance resources, and in recognition of the panoply of international affairs agencies operating today, the Budget proposes consolidating ADF and IAF's functions into USAID, as the U.S. Government's primary development agency. Through the consolidation, USAID would capitalize on the existing expertise, capacity, and tools that ADF and IAF provide, including their regional and market segment emphases, while offering these programs a platform that would bring organizational efficiencies and better align them with USAID's development programs, U.S. foreign policy objectives, and the National Security Strategy. The consolidation would continue to address congressional interest in small grant programs in Africa, Latin America, and the Caribbean, and also serve to elevate the small grants function as a development and diplomacy tool. At the same time, the consolidation would eliminate some redundancies and overhead, as well as streamline the number of agencies undertaking development work.

ELIMINATION: LEGAL SERVICES CORPORATION
Other Independent Agencies

The Budget proposes to end the one-size-fits-all model of providing legal services through a single Federal grant program, the Legal Services Corporation (LSC). This proposed elimination puts more control in the hands of State and local governments that better understand the needs of their communities.

Funding Summary
(In millions of dollars)

	2017 Enacted	2019 Request	2019 Change from 2017
Budget Authority..	385	18	-367

Justification

Established in the Legal Services Corporation Act of 1974, LSC is an independent 501(c)(3) nonprofit corporation that awards funding to legal services providers to promote civil legal assistance to low-income persons. The program supports mostly family law and housing matters, including evictions and foreclosures. This proposed elimination will encourage nonprofit organizations, businesses, law firms, and religious institutions to develop new models for providing legal aid, such as pro bono work, law school clinics, and innovative technologies. The proposal also puts more control in the hands of State and local governments that better understand the needs of their communities.

Further, LSC is not subject to the same accountability measures as other agencies, such as the Antideficiency Act and certain public reporting requirements, leading to potential areas of vulnerability in how Federal funds are ultimately disbursed.

LSC's own Office of Inspector General (OIG) has identified several instances of waste, fraud, and abuse involving grant recipients. In the October 2017 Semiannual Report to the Congress, the OIG reported a number of unallowable expenses incurred by grantees, including $17,896 in unjustified expenditures on floral arrangements, musical entertainment, and cake orders made as part of efforts to recruit private attorneys; multiple cases of unreasonable travel reimbursements for mileage between offices and personal residences; and unlawful bonuses derived from LSC funds for one grantee's chief operating officer.

The OIG further revealed allegations that employees from one grantee—including three members of the board of directors of a nonprofit entity—had participated in lobbying activities in violation of Federal regulations. This same nonprofit entity contracted with a registered lobbyist, who shared office space with the LSC grantee.

LSC's indefinite appropriation authorization expired in 1980.

ELIMINATION: NATIONAL ENDOWMENT FOR THE ARTS
Other Independent Agencies

The Budget proposes to eliminate Federal funding for the National Endowment for the Arts (NEA). Established in 1965, NEA uses partnerships with State arts agencies, other Federal agencies, and the philanthropic sector, to support arts learning, cultural heritage, and increasing access to the arts across the country. Forty percent of NEA funding is provided directly to State arts councils, with the remaining distributed as grants to theaters, libraries, schools, and non-profit organizations.

Funding Summary
(In millions of dollars)

	2017 Enacted	2019 Request	2019 Change from 2017
Budget Authority...	150	29	-121

Justification

The Budget proposes to begin shutting down NEA in 2019, given the notable funding support provided by private and other public sources and because the Administration does not consider NEA activities to be core Federal responsibilities. In 2014, NEA funding represented just four percent of total public and private support for the arts in the United States.

An *Open the Books* Oversight Report[1] found that NEA, the National Endowment for the Humanities, and the Institute for Museum and Library Services had provided grants in 2016 to over 70 nonprofit organizations that have asset bases larger than $1 billion.

Citations

[1] OpenTheBooks Oversight Report: *National Foundation on the Arts and Humanities, (2017).*

ELIMINATION: NATIONAL ENDOWMENT FOR THE HUMANITIES
Other Independent Agencies

The Budget proposes to eliminate Federal funding for the National Endowment for the Humanities (NEH). Established in 1965, NEH is intended to "serve and strengthen our Republic by promoting excellence in the humanities and conveying the lessons of history to all Americans." Nearly 33 percent of NEH funding is provided directly to State humanities councils, with the remaining distributed as grants to individuals, universities, libraries, museums, and schools.

Funding Summary
(In millions of dollars)

	2017 Enacted	2019 Request	2019 Change from 2017
Budget Authority...	150	42	-108

Justification

The Budget proposes to begin shutting down NEH in 2019, given there are non-Federal sources of funding for humanities and the Administration does not consider the activities within this agency to be core Federal responsibilities. Non-Federal funding for humanities in the United States comes from private donations from individuals, corporations, and foundations.

An *Open the Books* Oversight Report[1] found that NEH, the National Endowment for the Arts, and the Institute for Museum and Library Services had provided grants in 2016 to over 70 nonprofit organizations that have asset bases larger than $1 billion.

Citations

[1] OpenTheBooks Oversight Report: *National Foundation on the Arts and Humanities, (2017).*

ELIMINATION: NEIGHBORHOOD REINVESTMENT CORPORATION
Other Independent Agencies

The Budget proposes to end Federal support for the Neighborhood Reinvestment Corporation (NRC), commonly known as NeighborWorks, a statutorily chartered non-profit that receives the vast majority of its funding from Federal funds. A strong return on these funds has not been documented.

Funding Summary
(In millions of dollars)

	2017 Enacted	2019 Request	2019 Change from 2017
Budget Authority..	140	27	-113

Justification

NRC supports a network of local housing and community development organizations through grants, managerial oversight, and training. NRC is not a unique provider of housing and community services, and has been unable to document with evaluative rigor that its Federal funding leads to higher performance or better outcomes compared to the work of similar organizations. NRC's performance measurement system is largely a collection of output indicators rather than strong housing and community development outcomes. The production that members of the NRC network achieve comes largely from financial sources other than NRC.[1] Further, NRC has been unable to produce rigorous statistical evidence to link the provision of NRC's funding and technical support with improved outcomes.

The last year that NRC had an authorization for appropriations was 1994.

Citations

[1] NeighborWorks: *Community Report, http://www.neighborworks.org/About-Us/Community-Report*, (retrieved May 8, 2017).

ELIMINATION: REGIONAL COMMISSIONS
Other Independent Agencies

The Budget proposes to eliminate the Delta Regional Authority (DRA), the Denali Commission, and the Northern Border Regional Commission (NBRC), providing funding only for the orderly closure of the agencies. The Budget restores control over community and economic development efforts to State and local governments, and private entities.

Funding Summary
(In millions of dollars)

	2017 Enacted	2019 Request	2019 Change from 2017
Delta Regional Authority...	25	3	-22
Denali Commission...	17	7	-10
Northern Border Regional Commission..	10	1	-9

Justification

DRA, the Denali Commission, and NBRC are independent agencies that award Federal grants for regional development by funding infrastructure projects, workforce and economic development activities, and local capacity building efforts.

The Budget proposes to eliminate these commissions to reduce Federal spending and streamline the Federal Government's role, while encouraging States and localities to partner with the private sector to develop locally-tailored solutions to community problems. The majority of these regional commissions' activities are duplicative of other Federal programs, and their funding is set aside for special geographical designations rather than applied across the country based on objective criteria indicating local areas' levels of distress. For instance, the rationale for a unique and additional Federal subsidy to Alaska is difficult to justify given that the State of Alaska's oil revenues allow it to pay an annual dividend ($1,884 in 2017) to each of its residents.[1] Finally, the commissions' effectiveness at improving overall economic conditions in these areas remains unproven.

Citations

[1] State of Alaska Department of Revenue, Permanent Fund Dividend Division: *Annual Report 2017* (2017).

REDUCTION: U.S INSTITUTE OF PEACE
Other Independent Agencies

The Budget proposes to reduce Federal funding for the United States Institute of Peace (USIP), given its status as an independent nonprofit organization outside the Federal Government. The Budget assumes that USIP, like any other foreign assistance implementer, would have to compete for more of its funding through interagency agreements with other Federal agencies, rather than rely on its direct appropriation as its primary funding source.

Funding Summary
(In millions of dollars)

	2017 Enacted	2019 Request	2019 Change from 2017
Budget Authority..	38	20	-18

Justification

The Congress created USIP as an independent, non-profit corporation in 1984, but USIP's authorization for appropriations expired in 2015. The Administration is continuing its efforts to streamline functions across the Federal Government, particularly those that duplicate the efforts of other Federal programs or the non-profit and private sectors. Consistent with this goal, the Budget request for USIP would support the Institute's core operations and maintenance funding in 2019, but USIP would need to compete for funding for program work through increased interagency agreements with other Federal Government agencies. The Budget assumes that USIP would work closely with the Department of State, U.S. Agency for International Development, and the Department of Defense to leverage USIP's independence and flexibility to help those agencies accomplish their missions. This would be achieved through additional reimbursable agreements where USIP can serve as the program partner, while continuing to streamline USIP's operations and identifying opportunities for financial savings.

ELIMINATION: U.S. TRADE AND DEVELOPMENT AGENCY
Other Independent Agencies

The Budget proposes to eliminate funding for the U.S. Trade and Development Agency (TDA), given its mission is more appropriately served by the private sector. Since TDA is primarily focused on middle income countries, and not on development finance, TDA is not proposed for consolidation into the new Development Finance Institution (DFI). However, the DFI may have some tools similar to TDA's, such as feasibility studies, tailored for development finance purposes. The Administration's request of $12 million will allow TDA to conduct an orderly closeout of the Agency beginning in 2019, which includes sufficient funding for personnel, rent, program, and other closeout costs. No additional funding will be needed in 2020 and beyond.

Funding Summary
(In millions of dollars)

	2017 Enacted	2019 Request	2019 Change from 2017
Budget Authority	75	12	-63

Justification

TDA's dual mission is to support U.S. exports and jobs, while advancing infrastructure development in developing and middle-income countries. Its main programmatic focus is to support U.S. private sector participation in infrastructure projects in middle-income countries. However, many of these projects would likely proceed without TDA support and could thus be supported by the private sector without Government involvement. While the Administration wants U.S. businesses to invest in emerging markets to grow their businesses and create American jobs, these businesses have incentive to invest and should rely on private sector financing. In general, the United States should not provide taxpayer subsidies except in rare situations, such as when limited support is needed to offset inappropriate subsidies that disadvantage U.S. businesses. In fact, supporting select U.S. businesses over others puts the Government in the business of picking winners and losers, potentially distorting the free market.

ELIMINATION: WOODROW WILSON INTERNATIONAL CENTER FOR SCHOLARS
Other Independent Agencies

The Budget proposes to eliminate Federal funding for the Woodrow Wilson International Center for Scholars (the Center). The mission of the Center is to be a non-partisan policy forum and independent research institute for tackling global issues and to serve as the official living memorial for President Woodrow Wilson. Federal appropriations represent approximately one-third of total funding for the Center, which primarily relies on private donations for operations.

Funding Summary
(In millions of dollars)

	2017 Enacted	2019 Request	2019 Change from 2017
Budget Authority..	11	7	-4

Justification

As a living memorial, the Center works to achieve its mission by serving as a non-partisan policy forum, conducting independent research, and providing open dialogue to inform the policy community. This is achieved, in part, by hosting over 120 fellows from around the world each year who, along with staff, conduct research on policy issues confronting the United States, host public meetings and events, and undertake a wide range of outreach activities.

The Budget proposes to start phasing out the Center's Federal appropriation in 2019. The Center's Federal appropriation provides roughly one-third of its total annual funding, which indicates that it could continue to function in a somewhat more limited manner if the appropriation were eliminated.

The elimination of the Center's Federal appropriation would result in the Center relying on contracts and grants from public and non-public sources to support its continued operations, just like the dozens of other think tanks which operate in Washington, D.C. and around the country. The Administration believes that providing a direct appropriation to such an institution is not a core Federal Government mission. To conduct an orderly closeout of federally funded operations, the Budget requests $7.4 million in 2019.

MANDATORY REFORMS

CONDUCT SPECTRUM AUCTIONS BELOW 6 GIGAHERTZ
Multi-Agency

The Budget proposes to extend the Federal Communications Commission's (FCC) authority to conduct auctions.

Funding Summary
(In millions of dollars)

	2019	2020	2021	2022	2023	2024	2025	2026	2027	2028	2019-23	2019-28
Proposed Change from Current Law............................	0	-300	-300	0	0	0	0	0	0	-6,000	-600	-6,600

Justification

The Spectrum Pipeline Act of 2015 ("Act") requires the auction of 30 MHz of spectrum below 6 GHz by 2024, and extends the FCC's auction authority allowing for such auctions. Based on ongoing research authorized through the Act, the Administration anticipates that additional spectrum assignments will be made available for auction. As a result, the Budget proposes to extend the FCC's authority to conduct auctions to make any additional spectrum identified available for commercial use. Auction proceeds are expected to exceed $6 billion through 2028.

Additionally, following successful completion of the National Oceanic and Atmospheric Administration (NOAA) Spectrum Pipeline Plan, the Budget proposes that the FCC exercise auction authority to assign spectrum frequencies between 1675-1680 megahertz for wireless broadband use subject to sharing arrangements with Federal weather satellites. The proposal is expected to raise $600 million in receipts over 10 years.

ELIMINATE ALLOCATIONS TO THE HOUSING TRUST FUND AND CAPITAL MAGNET FUND
Multi-Agency

The Budget proposes to eliminate funding for the Housing Trust Fund and Capital Magnet Fund, two programs that provide Federal funding for affordable low-income housing. The Budget recognizes a greater role for State and local governments and the private sector in addressing affordable housing needs.

Funding Summary
(In millions of dollars)

	2019	2020	2021	2022	2023	2024	2025	2026	2027	2028	2019-23	2019-28
Proposed Change from Current Law..........................	-263	-158	-227	-296	-357	-385	-399	-419	-426	-433	-1,301	-3,363

Justification

The Housing Trust Fund, managed by the Department of Housing and Urban Development, provides grants to States to increase and preserve the supply of affordable housing primarily for extremely low-income families. The Capital Magnet Fund, managed by the Department of the Treasury's Community Development Financial Institutions (CDFI) Fund, provides grants to CDFIs and nonprofit housing organizations that are leveraged to finance affordable housing and related economic development activities. Originally established by the Housing and Economic Recovery Act of 2008 with dedicated funding from Fannie Mae and Freddie Mac assessments, a total of $627 million has been allocated to the funds since 2016.

Housing for low-income families is currently funded by multiple funding sources, including Federal, State, and local governments, as well as the private and nonprofit sectors. The result is a fragmented system with varying rules and regulations that create overlap and inefficiencies, as well as challenges to measuring collective performance.[1] The Budget would devolve some affordable housing activities to State and local governments who are better positioned to comprehensively address the array of unique market challenges, local policies, and impediments that lead to housing affordability problems.

Citations

[1] Government Accountability Office: *Affordable Rental Housing: Assistance Is Provided by Federal, State, and Local Programs, but There Is Incomplete Information on Collective Performance*, GAO-15-645, (September 2015).

REDUCE IMPROPER PAYMENTS AND OTHER PROGRAM INTEGRITY
Multi-Agency

By 2028, the Budget proposes to increase the prevention of improper payments through a series of actions to improve payment accuracy and financial performance over the budget horizon.

Funding Summary
(In millions of dollars)

	2019	2020	2021	2022	2023	2024	2025	2026	2027	2028	2019-23	2019-28
Reduce Improper Payments and Other Program Integrity Government-wide..................	-48	-1,678	-3,350	-5,572	-9,025	-10,900	-16,961	-28,262	-46,104	-65,740	-19,673	-187,640

Note: This total includes $158,381 million in savings from several proposals displayed in Table 10-3 of the Analytical Perspectives volume, and $29,259 million in savings from the Internal Revenue Service Cap Adjustment proposal shown in Table 10-2 of the Analytical Perspectives volume.

Justification

Addressing improper payments is necessary for legal compliance and the efficient use of financial resources. Even though the majority of Government payments are made properly, any waste of taxpayer money is unacceptable. The Budget prioritizes focusing on improper payments that result in a monetary loss to the government.

The Improper Payment Elimination and Recovery Act of 2010 defines an "improper payment" as any payment that should not have been made or that was made in an incorrect amount under statutory, contractual, administrative, or other legally applicable requirements. It is important to keep in mind that not all "improper payments" are the result of fraudulent actions or represent monetary loss to the Government.

In FY 2017, the Office of Management and Budget analyzed program-by-program improper payment data and concluded that it was more useful than aggregate improper payment data and in November 2017, PaymentAccuracy.gov was updated with this program-specific information, including the amount of improper payments that result in a monetary loss to the Government and the amount that does not.

Although approximately 90 programs reported improper payment estimates in FY 2017, four programs have significantly high payment error estimates. Executive Branch Agencies have ongoing interactions with their Inspectors General and the Government Accountability Office to improve payment integrity, with a specific focus on these four programs.

The Budget proposes savings associated with the President's promise to crack down on improper payments. Specifically, the Budget proposes to make significant investments in activities that ensure that taxpayer dollars are spent for purposes for which they were intended. For Example:

Unemployment Insurance Program Integrity Package—The Budget would reduce waste, fraud, and abuse in the Unemployment Insurance (UI) program with a package of program integrity proposals. These proposals would require States to use the tools already at their disposal for combating improper payments while expanding their authority to spend certain UI program funds on activities that reduce waste, fraud, and abuse in the system.

Reemployment Services and Eligibility Assessments—The Budget proposes to expand Reemployment Services and Eligibility Assessments, an evidence based activity that saves an average of $536 per claimant in UI benefit costs by reducing improper payments and getting claimants back to work more quickly and at higher wages. The Budget proposes to create a permanent program that would allow each State to provide these services to one half of its UI claimants as well as all of its transitioning service members.

Improve collection of pension information from States and localities—The Budget proposes a data collection approach designed to provide seed money to the States for them to develop systems that would enable them to report pension payment information to the Social Security Administration. The proposal would improve reporting for non-covered pensions by including up to $70 million for administrative expenses, $50 million of which would be available to the States, to develop a mechanism so that the Social Security Administration (SSA) can enforce the current law offsets for the Windfall Elimination Provision and Government Pension Offset, which are a major source of improper payments. The proposal would save $8.86 billion over 10 years.

Increase oversight of paid tax preparers—Paid tax return preparers have an important role in tax administration because they assist taxpayers in complying with their obligations under the tax laws. Incompetent and dishonest tax return preparers increase collection costs, reduce revenues, disadvantage taxpayers by potentially subjecting them to penalties and interest as a result of incorrect returns, and undermine confidence in the tax system. To promote high quality services from paid tax return preparers, the proposal would explicitly provide that the Secretary of the Treasury has the authority to regulate all paid tax return preparers.

Provide more flexible authority for the Internal Revenue Service (IRS) to address correctable errors—The Administration proposes to expand IRS authority to correct errors on taxpayer returns. Current statute only allows the IRS to correct errors on returns in certain limited instances, such as basic math errors or the failure to include the appropriate social security number or taxpayer identification number. This proposal would expand the instances in which the IRS could correct a taxpayer's return including cases where: (1) the information provided by the taxpayer does not match the information contained in Government databases; (2) the taxpayer has exceeded the lifetime limit for claiming a deduction or credit; or (3) the taxpayer has failed to include with his or her return, certain documentation that is required by statute.

IRS Program Integrity Cap Adjustment—The Administration proposes to establish and fund a new adjustment to the discretionary caps for IRS program integrity activities starting in 2019. The IRS base funding within the discretionary caps funds current tax administration activities, including all tax enforcement and compliance program activities, in the Enforcement and Operations Support accounts. The additional $362 million cap adjustment in 2019 will fund new and continuing investments in expanding and improving the effectiveness and efficiency of the IRS's tax enforcement program. The activities are estimated to generate $44 billion in additional revenue over 10 years and cost approximately $15 billion resulting in an estimated net savings of $29 billion. Once the new staff are trained and become fully operational these initiatives are expected to generate roughly $4 in additional revenue for every $1 in IRS expenses. Notably, the return on investment is likely understated because it only includes amounts received; it does not reflect the effect enhanced enforcement has on deterring noncompliance. This indirect deterrence helps to ensure the continued payment of over $3 trillion in taxes paid each year without direct enforcement measures.

Hold fraud facilitators liable for overpayments—The Budget proposes to hold fraud facilitators liable for overpayments by allowing SSA to recover the overpayment from a third party if the third party was responsible for making fraudulent statements or providing false evidence that allowed the beneficiary to receive payments that should not have been paid. This proposal would result in an estimated $6 million in savings over 10 years.

Government wide use of Customs and Border Protection (CBP) entry/exit data to prevent improper payments—The Budget proposes the use of CBP Entry/Exit data to prevent improper Old-Age, Survivors, and Disability Insurance Program (OASDI) and Supplemental Security Insurance (SSI) payments. Generally, U.S. citizens can receive benefits regardless of residence. Non-citizens may be subject to additional residence requirements depending on the country of residence and benefit type. However, an SSI beneficiary who is outside the United States for 30 consecutive days is not eligible for benefits for that month. These data have the potential to be useful across the Government to prevent improper payments. This proposal would result in an estimated $183 million in savings over 10 years.

Allow SSA to use commercial databases to verify real property in the SSI Program—The Budget proposes to reduce improper payments and lessen recipients' reporting burden by authorizing SSA to use private commercial databases to check for ownership of real property (i.e. land and buildings), which could affect SSI eligibility. Consent to allow SSA to access these databases would be a condition of benefit receipt for new beneficiaries and current beneficiaries who complete a determination. All other current due process and appeal rights would be preserved. This proposal would result in savings of $604 million over 10 years.

Authorize SSA to use all collection tools to recover funds in certain scenarios—The Budget also proposes to allow SSA a broader range of collection tools when someone improperly receives a benefit after the beneficiary has died. Currently, if a spouse cashes a benefit payment (or does not return a directly deposited benefit) for an individual who has died and the spouse is also not receiving benefits on that individual's record, SSA has more limited collection tools available than would be the case if the spouse also receives benefits on the deceased individual's earning record. The Budget proposal would end this disparate treatment of similar types of improper payments and results in an estimated $45 million in savings over 10 years.

Additional debt collection authority for SSA civil monetary penalties assessments—This proposal would assist SSA with ensuring the integrity of its programs and increase SSA recoveries by establishing statutory authority for the SSA to use the same debt collection tools available for recovery of delinquent overpayments toward recovery of delinquent CMP and assessments.

Exclude SSA debts from discharge in bankruptcy—The debts due to an overpayment of Social Security benefits are generally dischargeable in bankruptcy. The Budget includes a proposal to exclude such debts from discharge in bankruptcy, except when it would result in an undue hardship. This proposal would help ensure program integrity by increasing the amount of overpayments SSA recovers and would save $275 million over the 2019 through 2028 window.

Increase the overpayment collection threshold for OASDI—The Budget would change the minimum monthly withholding amount for recovery of Social Security benefit overpayments to reflect the increase in the average monthly benefit since the Agency established the current minimum of $10 in 1960. By changing this amount from $10 to 10 percent of the monthly benefit payable, SSA would recover overpayments more quickly and better fulfill its stewardship obligations to the combined Social Security Trust Funds. The SSI program already utilizes the 10 percent rule. Debtors could still pay less if the negotiated amount would allow for repayment of the debt in 36 months. If the beneficiary cannot afford to have his or her full benefit payment withheld because he or she cannot meet ordinary and necessary living expenses, the beneficiary may request partial withholding. To determine a proper partial withholding amount, SSA negotiates (as well as re-negotiates at the overpaid beneficiary's request) a partial withholding rate. This proposal would result in savings of almost $1.4 billion over 10 years.

Simplify the Supplemental Security Income (SSI) Program—The Budget proposes to simplify the SSI program as a part of a package of proposals to reform disability insurance programs. Additional information on this proposal is included in the *Reform Federal Disability Programs* section of this volume.

Medicare, Medicaid, and Children's Health Insurance Program (CHIP) Program Integrity Proposals—The Budget includes a robust package of Medicare, Medicaid, and CHIP program integrity proposals to help prevent fraud and abuse before they occur; detect fraud and abuse as early as possible; provide greater flexibility to the Secretary of Health and Human Services to implement program integrity activities that allow for efficient use of resources and achieve high return-on-investment; and promote integrity in Federal-State financing. Additional information on Medicare program integrity proposals are included in the *Medicare: Address Fraud and Abuse* section of this volume. Additional information on Medicaid and CHIP program integrity proposals are included in the *Medicaid: Address Wasteful Spending, Fraud, and Abuse* section of the MSV.

There is compelling evidence that investments in administrative resources can significantly decrease the rate of improper payments and recoup many times their initial investment. Combating improper payments resulting in a monetary loss within the Federal Government is a top priority for this Administration. This Administration will continue to explore new and groundbreaking ways to address the problem. Additional program integrity and improper payment proposals are found in the Budget Process chapter in the Analytical Perspectives volume.

REFORM FEDERAL DISABILITY PROGRAMS
Multi-Agency

The Budget proposes changes to the Supplemental Security Income (SSI) program, building on the FY 2018 Budget efforts to reform disability insurance programs to promote greater labor force participation (LFP) and to reduce inefficiency in Government programs. The two primary components include targeted changes in the SSI Youth program and the simplification of the SSI program in general. Related proposals address inequities in the system, close loopholes that make the program susceptible to fraud, and remove unnecessary administrative burdens.

Funding Summary
(In millions of dollars)

	2019	2020	2021	2022	2023	2024	2025	2026	2027	2028	2019-23	2019-28
Improve SSI Youth Transition to Work..................	-5	-28	6	46	21	-6	-35	-59	-80	-108	40	-248
Simplify administration of the SSI program..................	0	-347	-86	-68	-50	-29	-18	-6	6	19	-551	-579
Test new approaches to increase labor force participation..................	100	100	100	100	100	-2,384	-5,070	-9,171	-13,610	-18,632	500	-48,367
Reduce 12 month retroactive DI benefits to six months.......	-362	-669	-846	-992	-1,057	-1,126	-1,198	-1,268	-1,337	-1,401	-3,926	-10,256
Create a sliding scale for multi-recipient SSI families.....	-588	-618	-636	-693	-661	-631	-702	-720	-738	-814	-3,196	-6,801
Offset overlapping unemployment and disability payments..................	0	-81	-209	-255	-281	-296	-311	-325	-343	-356	-826	-2,457
Reinstate the reconsideration review stage in 10 states.......	91	-76	-295	-424	-362	-354	-420	-469	-519	-579	-1,066	-3,407
Eliminate Workers Compensation Reverse Offset..................	0	0	-22	-22	-23	-25	-26	-28	-30	-31	-67	-207
Change the representative fee and approval process............	0	3	16	29	43	41	45	44	44	45	91	310
Eliminate the requirement for representative payees to provide an annual accounting report..................	0	0	0	0	0	0	0	0	0	0	0	0
Implement Administrative Law Judge (ALJ) reforms.............	0	0	0	0	0	0	0	0	0	0	0	0
Total..................	-764	-1,716	-1,972	-2,279	-2,270	-4,810	-7,735	-12,002	-16,607	-21,857	-9,001	-72,012

Justification

Improve SSI youth transition to work—The SSI transition-age (ages 14 to 25) youth population, despite their disabilities, should have equal opportunities as they become adults to work and achieve self-sufficiency. Unfortunately, a majority of each new generation of SSI youth move directly onto the adult SSI program at age 18 and those who do not remain on SSI (approximately 40 percent) have lives marked by low LFP in adulthood and persistent poverty. In particular, the Budget proposes three areas of reform to improve the life outcomes and connect SSI youth to work.

First, the Budget would better identify medical improvement at the earliest point to increase oversight and signal the importance of SSI youth investing in their education and development. The Budget proposes to (a) institute age 6 and 12 initial disability reviews and (b) increase the frequency and effectiveness of continuing disability reviews (CDRs) by expanding the CDR diary system for all disability beneficiaries from three to four categories, allowing the Social Security Administration (SSA) to conduct CDRs more frequently for those medical impairments that are expected or likely to improve.

Second, the Budget would improve SSI youth work incentives by eliminating administrative barriers and increasing the value of work by proposing to disregard all earned income and eliminate income reporting requirements through age 20, provide a higher disregard of earnings with a gradual phase-down for SSI recipients between ages 21 and 25, and eliminate school enrollment reporting requirements.

Finally, the Budget would improve access to vocational rehabilitation services for SSI transition age youth by allowing SSA to make referrals to these services.

Simplify administration of the SSI program—The Budget proposes changes to simplify the SSI program by incentivizing support from recipients' family and friends, reducing the Social Security Administration's (SSA) administrative burden, and streamlining requirements for applicants. SSI benefits are reduced by the amount of food and shelter, or in-kind support and maintenance, a beneficiary receives. The policy is burdensome to administer and is a leading source of SSI improper payments. The Budget proposes to replace the complex calculation of in-kind support and maintenance with a flat rate reduction for adults living with other adults to capture economies of scale. The Budget also proposes to eliminate dedicated accounts for past due benefits and to eliminate the administratively burdensome consideration whether a couple is holding themselves out as married.

Test new approaches to increase labor force participation—The Budget proposes to evaluate creative and effective ways to promote greater LFP of people with disabilities by expanding demonstration authority that allows SSA, in collaboration with other agencies, to test new program rules and require mandatory participation by program applicants and beneficiaries. Potential applicants and beneficiaries have a wide range of conditions and experiences; mandatory participation is required in order to accurately assess how program changes might affect different groups of people. Promising projects that require mandatory participation for this proposal include: test "time limited benefits" for beneficiaries for a period when they would be more likely to return to work; require applicants to engage in job seeking activities before their application is considered; and mandate that lower back pain and arthritis sufferers engage in rehabilitation traditionally used in occupational health treatment services before receiving benefits. An expert panel will identify specific changes to program rules that would increase LFP and reduce program participation, informed by successful demonstration results and other evidence.

Reduce 12 month retroactive DI benefits to six months—New disability insurance (DI) beneficiaries are eligible for up to 12 months of benefits before the date of their application, depending upon the date they became disabled. This proposal would reduce retroactivity for disabled workers, which is the same policy already in effect for individuals receiving retirement benefits. This proposal will not modify retroactivity for Medicare eligibility.

Create a sliding scale for multi-recipient SSI families—Currently, multi-recipient SSI families are eligible to receive an equal full benefit amount for each SSI child recipient. However, economies of scale in some types of consumption such as housing reduce per capita living expenses, so that two children generally do not need twice the income as one child. Federal poverty guidelines and other means-tested benefits take into account these efficiencies. The Budget proposes to create a sliding scale family maximum for SSI disability benefits that considers the number of additional family recipients. It would keep the maximum benefit for one recipient the same as in current law but equally reduce the maximum amount for all eligible children and parents in the same family for each additional recipient.

Offset overlapping unemployment and disability payments—The Budget proposes to close a loophole that allows individuals to receive unemployment insurance (UI) and DI for the same period of joblessness. The proposal would offset the DI benefit to account for concurrent receipt of UI benefits. Under current law, concurrent receipt of DI benefits and unemployment compensation is allowable. UI is intended to compensate individuals for short-term bouts of unemployment while they look to return to work while DI is intended to compensate individuals who cannot return to work on a long-term basis due to a disability, allowing double dipping that is unnecessary and wasteful.

Reinstate the reconsideration review application stage in 10 States—The Budget proposes reinstating reconsideration in 10 States, conforming these States with the practices used in the rest of the Nation. This reform requires a second review by the State Disability Determination Services (DDS) before an appeal goes to an Administrative Law Judge (ALJ). Other States already require disability applicants to have their claim "reconsidered" before they can appeal to an ALJ.

Eliminate Workers' Compensation (WC) reverse offset—The Budget proposes to eliminate reverse offsets in 15 States where WC benefits are offset instead of DI benefits. Currently, in most States, the combination of benefits from WC and DI is limited to 80 percent of the recipient's earnings before they were disabled. If necessary, DI benefits are usually offset to meet the limit. However, 15 States currently reduce the benefit from WC rather than DI in order to achieve the 80 percent limit, creating an unjustified inequity across States. This option would eliminate the reverse offsets in these States.

Change the representative fee and approval process—This proposal relieves SSA of responsibility for fee approval, withholding, and payment functions; however, it would not affect SSA's ability to prescribe who may and may not represent claimants. This proposal would streamline and decrease SSA's operations and hearings workloads, allowing employees to focus on adjudicating more cases and completing other high priority workloads, thereby better serving the public.

Eliminate the requirement for representative payees to provide an annual accounting report—SSA is currently required to obtain an annual accounting report for approximately 8 million beneficiaries each year. As a result, SSA is obligated to send, track, and analyze annual accounting reports, which requires a high level of administrative effort. This proposal eliminates the statutory requirement for annual payee accounting for minor children and spouses, which accounts for about half of all payee accounting.

Implement ALJ reforms—The ALJ system is in need of additional flexibility. Currently ALJs are hired for an indefinite period and without a probationary period. They also enjoy very substantial protections from disciplinary actions. Once hired, ALJs are very difficult to remove. However, there have been recent cases where an ALJ was hired, and it became clear that the individual would be unsuccessful at the job. Additionally, some agencies experience workload surges where an influx of ALJ talent is needed for a specific period of time, but not thereafter. This proposal would increase flexibility in ALJ hiring and discipline, by among other things, introducing probationary periods for newly hired ALJs and permitting the hiring of ALJs for limited terms to address variations in agency workflow. The proposed change would also allow the faster removal of ALJs who commit misconduct and ensure the proper appointment of ALJs.

REFORM MEDICAL LIABILITY
Multi-Agency

The Budget proposes to reform medical liability beginning in 2019. The reforms are expected to reduce healthcare costs and health insurance premiums by reducing medical liability insurance premiums and defensive medicine practices. Under this proposal, Federal health program costs would decrease (including in Medicare, Medicaid, and the Federal Employee Health Benefits Program) and taxable income and payroll tax receipts would increase.

Funding Summary
(In millions of dollars)

	2019	2020	2021	2022	2023	2024	2025	2026	2027	2028	2019-23	2019-28
Proposed Change from Current Law............................	-178	-712	-1,862	-3,253	-4,552	-6,098	-7,783	-8,614	-9,122	-9,945	-10,557	-52,119

Justification

The current medical liability system does not work for patients or providers, nor does it promote high quality, evidence-based care. Providers practice with a threat of potentially frivolous lawsuits, and injured patients often do not receive just compensation for their injuries. The Budget proposes to reform medical liability and reduce defensive medicine beginning in 2019 by implementing a set of provisions to reduce the number of high dollar awards, limit liability, reduce provider burden, promote evidence-based practices, and strengthen the physician-patient relationship. Specifically, the Budget proposal includes: a cap on non-economic damage awards of $250,000 (increasing with inflation over time); a three-year statute of limitations; allowing courts to modify attorney's fee arrangements; allowing evidence of a claimant's payments from other sources (e.g., workers' compensation, auto insurance) to be introduced at trial; creating a safe harbor for clinicians following evidence-based clinical practice guidelines; and authorizing the Secretary to provide guidance to States to create expert panels and administrative health care tribunals to review medical liability cases.

REPEAL AND REPLACE OBAMACARE
Multi-Agency

Obamacare has destabilized the individual insurance market, shifted control over health care decisions from consumers and States to the Federal Government, and increased premiums for millions of individuals. To address these failures, the Budget supports a two-part approach to repealing and replacing Obamacare, starting with enactment of legislation modeled closely after the Graham-Cassidy-Heller-Johnson (GCHJ) bill as soon as possible. The second part of the Budget proposal includes additional reforms to address unsustainable healthcare spending trends and builds upon the GCHJ bill to make the system more efficient. This includes proposals to align the growth rates for the Market-Based Health Care Grant Program and Medicaid per capita cap and block grant with the Consumer Price Index (CPI-U). This two-part approach ensures States have the financial support they need to transition away from Obamacare and its Medicaid expansion while allowing greater choice and competition in health care markets and more sustainable Government health spending over the long-term.

Funding Summary
(In millions of dollars)

	2019	2020	2021	2022	2023	2024	2025	2026	2027	2028	2019-23	2019-28
PROPOSAL MODELED AFTER THE GCHJ BILL.......	12,257	73,844	12,433	9,994	12,634	12,835	6,624	-11,187	-13,380	-25,476	121,162	90,578
Medicaid reforms.................	-2,885	-67,165	-92,350	-98,060	-104,475	-112,350	-126,155	-140,800	-159,945	-179,385	-364,935	-1,083,570
Market Based Health Care Grant Program......................	0	146,000	146,000	157,000	168,000	179,000	190,000	190,000	210,000	220,000	617,000	1,606,000
Revenues...................	3,452	8,617	2,503	2,829	2,883	2,959	3,192	3,473	3,676	4,092	20,284	37,676
Other savings, net................	11,690	-13,608	-43,720	-51,775	-53,774	-56,774	-60,413	-63,860	-67,111	-70,183	-151,187	-469,528
ADDITIONAL DEFICIT REDUCTION......................	-9,000	-50,750	-39,400	-51,337	-68,908	-85,958	-98,940	-101,353	-123,890	-135,748	-219,395	-765,284
Market Based Health Care Grant Program......................	0	-26,000	-23,240	-31,417	-39,528	-47,573	-55,550	-52,458	-69,295	-76,058	-120,185	-421,119
Medicaid reforms..................	0	-4,500	-11,410	-19,920	-28,630	-37,635	-42,640	-48,145	-53,845	-58,940	-64,460	-305,665
State implementation.............	1,000	750	250	0	0	0	0	0	0	0	2,000	2,000
Other savings, net................	-10,000	-21,000	-5,000	0	-750	-750	-750	-750	-750	-750	-36,750	-40,500
Total.......................................	3,257	23,094	-26,967	-41,343	-56,274	-73,123	-92,316	-112,540	-137,270	-161,224	-98,233	-674,706

Justification

Average premiums increased 105 percent from 2013 to 2017 while choices have dwindled. In 2017, people in one-third of counties only had a single insurer from which to purchase a plan on an exchange. For 2018, approximately 30 percent of enrollees only had choices from a single insurer.[1] The Exchanges have not done enough to attract healthier individuals and families that want affordable options that meet their needs. Additionally, the Affordable Care Act's Medicaid expansion has cost significantly more than expected. For example, in 2015, Actuaries from the Centers for Medicare and Medicaid Services increased their estimates of federal spending for the average Medicaid expansion enrollee in that year by 50 percent.[2] Overall, the cost per newly insured individual is far more than was expected. To address these failures, the Budget supports a two-part approach to repealing and replacing Obamacare that couples a slightly modified GCHJ bill with additional reforms to help set Government healthcare spending on a sustainable fiscal path that will lead to higher value spending.

The first of this two-part approach is to enact GCHJ as soon as possible, with a modification to delay elimination of the Public Health Prevention Fund (PPHF) until 2020. The Market-Based Health Care Grant Program in the GCHJ bill would provide more equitable and sustainable funding to States to develop affordable healthcare options. The block grant program will promote structural reforms to improve the functioning of the health care market through greater choice and competition, with States and consumers in charge rather than the Washington bureaucracy. The Budget would allow States to use the block grant for a variety of approaches in order to help their residents, including those with high cost medical needs and former Medicaid expansion enrollees, afford quality health care services. This part of the two-part proposal is estimated to cost approximately $90.6 billion over 2019-2028. This is the first time the Administration has scored this legislation. Previous scores for legislative purposes would likely have included significant savings attributable to repealing Obamacare's individual mandate which may have resulted in net savings for the bill. Since that time, however, the Congress repealed the mandate, which was an important first step in relieving American's from the failures of Obamacare. The impact of that repeal is reflected in the baseline for the 2019 Budget.

Current growth in Medicaid spending is unsustainable, with growth outpacing gross domestic product and national health spending and accounting for an increasing share of Federal and State budgets.[3] The current open-ended structure of Federal Medicaid funding encourages States to shift costs to the Federal Government and does not encourage States to focus on preventing waste, fraud, and abuse. At the State level, Medicaid crowds out important State priorities such as investments in education, public safety, and infrastructure. Medicaid's outdated rules are restrictive and complex, tying States' hands and preventing States from designing innovative approaches that address the specific needs of their populations. This is why the President is committed to the comprehensive Medicaid reform in the GCHJ bill. This reform includes the repeal of the Obamacare Medicaid expansion and modernization of Medicaid financing. It will give States the choice between a per capita cap and a block grant with the goal of empowering States to design individual, State-based solutions that prioritize Medicaid dollars for the most vulnerable and support innovations such as community engagement initiatives for able-bodied adults.

National healthcare spending trends are unsustainable in the long term. The second part of the proposal in the Budget aims to reverse these trends and includes additional reforms to build upon the GCHJ bill to make the system more efficient, including proposals to align the Market-Based Health Care Grant Program, Medicaid per capita cap and block grant growth rates with the Consumer Price Index (CPI-U), a metric more in line with historical pre-Obamacare Medicaid per enrollee spending growth that will lead to sustainable long-term spending. This proposal would also provide implementation funding to support States' efforts to implement their new programs.

Citations

[1] Department of Health and Human Services Office of the Assistant Secretary for Planning and Evaluation: *Health Plan Choice and Premiums in the 2018 Federal Health Insurance Exchange*, (October 2017).

[2] Department of Health and Human Services Centers for Medicare & Medicaid Services, Office of the Actuary: *2015 Actuarial Report on the Financial Outlook for Medicaid*, (2015).

[3] National Association of State Budget Officers: *Fiscal Survey of the States*, (Fall 2017).

ELIMINATE FOOD FOR PROGRESS FOOD AID PROGRAM
Department of Agriculture

The Budget proposes to eliminate the Food for Progress (FFPr) program because development expertise is concentrated in other agencies, most notably the U.S. Agency for International Development (USAID), which can administer development programs at a much lower cost than FFPr. The FFPr program provides for the donation of U.S. commodities to developing countries. U.S. agricultural commodities donated to recipient countries are sold in the local or third-country markets generally at a significant loss to U.S. taxpayers and the cash proceeds of those sales are used to fund programs that aim to improve agricultural productivity in the recipient county.

Funding Summary
(In millions of dollars)

	2019	2020	2021	2022	2023	2024	2025	2026	2027	2028	2019-23	2019-28
Proposed Change from Current Law...........................	-166	-166	-166	-166	-166	-166	-166	-166	-166	-166	-830	-1,660

Justification

International development programs are better aligned with the USAID mission and expertise. The USAID mission highlights international development and humanitarian responses while the U.S. Department of Agriculture (USDA) mission highlights domestic agricultural production. In line with its mission, USAID seeks to use food aid to address humanitarian objectives, while USDA uses U.S. food aid programs to subsidize American farmers.

According to a 2011 Government Accountability Office report, FFPr monetizes food aid shipments, i.e., it ships and sells U.S. commodities abroad -- generally at a loss of 42 percent and uses the proceeds to fund development programs.[1] That is, when USDA buys and delivers a dollar of U.S. food abroad and then sells it to raise proceeds for its development programs, the receipts typically average only 58 cents, for a loss to U.S. taxpayers of 42 cents.

The amount of U.S. commodities purchased by FFPr is a negligible portion of U.S. agricultural production and exports. In 2016, FFPr spent approximately $116 million on U.S. commodities, roughly 0.03 percent of U.S. agricultural production or 0.09 percent of U.S. agricultural exports.

There are other more effective ways that USDA can support U.S. farmers using its expertise in agriculture, while USAID can use its expertise to most effectively prioritize and implement international development and humanitarian assistance programs. In addition to USAID's central role in humanitarian assistance, USAID administers and directly funds the main bilateral longer-term international agricultural development and food security program for the U.S. Government.

Citations

[1] Government Accountability Office, International Food Assistance: *Funding Development Projects through the Purchase, Shipment, and Sale of U.S. Commodities Is Inefficient and Can Cause Adverse Market Impacts*, GAO-11-636, (June 2011).

ELIMINATE INTEREST PAYMENTS TO ELECTRIC AND TELECOMMUNICATIONS UTILITIES
Department of Agriculture

The Budget proposes to eliminate the interest accrual on future deposits in the Rural Utilities Service borrowers' *cushion of credit* accounts. The program is unnecessary since rural electric and telecommunications cooperatives can find comparable investment options in the private sector.

Funding Summary
(In millions of dollars)

	2019	2020	2021	2022	2023	2024	2025	2026	2027	2028	2019-23	2019-28
Proposed Change from Current Law.........................	-129	-127	-130	-130	-128	-129	-129	-129	-129	-129	-644	-1,289

Justification

The *cushion of credit* program was authorized in 1987 as part of an omnibus reconciliation package. It set up a program to encourage rural electric and telecommunications borrowers to repay their Rural Utilities Service (RUS) debt. Under the program, borrowers make voluntary deposits into *cushion of credit* accounts and use those deposits to make their scheduled payments on loans made or guaranteed by RUS. The borrower earns interest on these deposits at a rate of five percent. When the program was authorized, the prime interest rate averaged 8.28 percent[1], now it is 4.5 percent.[2] The intent of the program was not to guarantee a higher income from the special interest rate. Rural electric and telecommunications utility borrowers do not need these unique interest payments to guarantee loan repayment, especially when the private sector offers comparable investment options.

Citations

[1] Forecast-Chart: *Historical Prime Rate,* http://www.forecast-chart.com/interest-prime-interest.html, (Retrieved Jan. 12, 2018).

[2] Bankrate: *Prime rate, federal funds rate, COFI,* https://www.bankrate.com/rates/interest-rates/prime-rate.aspx, (Retrieved Jan. 12, 2018).

ELIMINATE THE RURAL ECONOMIC DEVELOPMENT PROGRAM
Department of Agriculture

The Budget proposes to eliminate the interest accrual on future deposits in the Rural Utilities Service borrowers' *cushion of credit* accounts, including the interest that is paid to the Rural Economic Development Grant account to pay for rural economic grants and loans. This change is consistent with other Budget proposals that eliminate rural business programs.

Funding Summary
(In millions of dollars)

	2019	2020	2021	2022	2023	2024	2025	2026	2027	2028	2019-23	2019-28
Proposed Change from Current Law............................		-158	-160	0	0	0	0	0	0	0	-318	-318

Justification

Year after year, the Government Accountability Office includes the Rural Business & Cooperative Service (RBS) in its annual report on fragmentation, overlap, and duplication, and the Department of Agriculture's (USDA) Inspector General found two of the Agency's largest loan and grant programs to be improperly managed. RBS programs lack program evaluation, so it has not been possible to assess program impact. USDA has not been able to demonstrate that these programs meet the broader goals of reducing rural poverty, out-migration, or unemployment.

The Administration's tax, regulatory, and infrastructure policies are expected to be more effective at improving rural economies and job growth.

ESTABLISH AGRICULTURAL MARKETING SERVICE USER FEE
Department of Agriculture

The Administration proposes establishing an Agricultural Marketing Service (AMS) user fee to cover the full costs of the Agency's oversight of Marketing Orders and Agreements.

Funding Summary
(In millions of dollars)

	2019	2020	2021	2022	2023	2024	2025	2026	2027	2028	2019-23	2019-28
Proposed Change from Current Law..........................	-20	-20	-20	-20	-20	-20	-20	-20	-20	-20	-100	-200

Justification

Marketing Orders and Agreements are initiated by industry to help provide stable markets, and are tailored to the specific industry's needs. For example, Marketing Orders and Agreements for fruits, vegetables, and other specialty crops help control supply and ensure that produce on the market maintains high-quality standards. AMS is authorized only to provide oversight of Marketing Orders and Agreements. AMS oversight responsibilities range from reviewing applications for new orders and holding hearings on proposals, to publishing Federal Register notices establishing new agreements. The industries that substantially benefit from Marketing Orders and Agreements should pay for the oversight of these programs.

ESTABLISH ANIMAL AND PLANT HEALTH INSPECTION SERVICE USER FEE
Department of Agriculture

The Budget proposes establishing three new Animal and Plant Health Inspection Service (APHIS) user fees to offset costs related to 1) enforcement of the Animal Welfare Act; 2) regulation of biotechnology derived products; and 3) regulation of veterinary biologics products. The fees would cover costs related to licenses, registration, and authorization for regulated entities.

Funding Summary
(In millions of dollars)

	2019	2020	2021	2022	2023	2024	2025	2026	2027	2028	2019-23	2019-28
Proposed Change from Current Law...............	-23	-23	-23	-23	-23	-23	-23	-23	-23	-23	-115	-230

Justification

Under the authority of the Animal Welfare Act (AWA), APHIS conducts activities designed to ensure the humane care and treatment of certain animals bred for commercial sale, used in research, transported commercially or exhibited to the public. These activities include licensing, registering, and inspecting certain establishments to ensure compliance with the AWA. APHIS would charge entities for the costs associated with licensing and registration.

Under the authority of the Plant Protection Act, APHIS regulates the importation, interstate movement, and field-testing of organisms derived through biotechnology that may pose a plant pest risk. After careful review, APHIS may issue a permit or notification to allow entities to conduct these specific activities, and conduct the necessary oversight to ensure compliance. APHIS would charge an application fee from entities seeking authorization for the introduction of biotechnology derived products.

Under the authority of the Virus-Serum-Toxin Act, APHIS regulates veterinary biologics (vaccines, bacteria, antisera, diagnostic kits, and other products of biological origin) to ensure that those products produced in or imported into the United States are not "worthless, contaminated, dangerous, or harmful." APHIS' licensing activities allow manufacturers to market their products. APHIS would charge a licensing fee to manufacturers of veterinary biologics.

ESTABLISH FOOD SAFETY AND INSPECTION SERVICE USER FEE
Department of Agriculture

The Budget proposes establishing a Food Safety and Inspection Service (FSIS) user fee to cover the costs of all domestic inspection activity, import re-inspection, and most of the central operations costs for Federal, State, and international inspection programs for meat, poultry, and eggs.

Funding Summary
(In millions of dollars)

	2019	2020	2021	2022	2023	2024	2025	2026	2027	2028	2019-23	2019-28
Proposed Change from Current Law............................	0	-660	-660	-660	-660	-660	-660	-660	-660	-660	-2,640	-5,940

Justification

FSIS inspections benefit the meat, poultry, and egg industries. FSIS personnel are continuously present for all egg processing and domestic slaughter operations, inspect each livestock and poultry carcass, and inspect operations at meat and poultry processing establishments at least once per shift. The inspections cover microbiological and chemical testing, as well as cleanliness and cosmetic product defects. The "inspected by USDA" stamp on meat and poultry labels provides industry with a special government service which justifies their payment because this increases consumer confidence, potentially increasing sales. The proposed user fee would not apply to Federal functions such as investigation, enforcement, risk analysis, and emergency response. The Administration estimates this fee would increase the cost of meat, poultry, and eggs for consumers by less than one cent per pound.

ESTABLISH PACKERS AND STOCKYARDS PROGRAM USER FEE
Department of Agriculture

The Budget proposes establishing a Packers and Stockyards Program User Fee to recover costs for the licensing of livestock market agencies, dealers, stockyards, packers, and swine contractors.

Funding Summary
(In millions of dollars)

	2019	2020	2021	2022	2023	2024	2025	2026	2027	2028	2019-23	2019-28
Proposed Change from Current Law..........................	-23	-23	-23	-23	-23	-23	-23	-23	-23	-23	-115	-230

Justification

The proposed fee would cover costs of the Packers and Stockyards Program, which benefits the livestock, meat, and poultry industries by promoting fair business practices and competitive market environments. Taxpayers should not be required to subsidize a benefit that is targeted to industry.

FARM BILL SAVINGS
Department of Agriculture

The Budget proposes to maintain a strong safety-net for farmers while achieving savings by eliminating subsidies to higher income farmers, reducing overly generous crop insurance subsidies to producers and companies, and by eliminating some programs that have no Federal purpose. The Budget proposes to: limit commodity, crop insurance, and conservation assistance to producers that have an Adjusted Gross Income (AGI) of $500,000 or less; reduce premium subsidies for crop insurance from an average subsidy rate of 62 percent to 48 percent; reduce payments made to private sector insurance companies; tighten commodity payment limits; and better target conservation funding to the most sensitive agricultural land.

Funding Summary
(In millions of dollars)

	2019	2020	2021	2022	2023	2024	2025	2026	2027	2028	2019-23	2019-28
Limit Eligibility for Agricultural Commodity Payments to $500,000 (AGI)	-114	-89	-142	-135	-124	-120	-111	-102	-98	-90	-604	-1,125
Limit Crop Insurance Eligibility to $500,000 AGI	0	-56	-58	-67	-71	-77	-84	-92	-102	-117	-252	-724
Limit Crop Insurance Premium Subsidies	0	-2,231	-2,258	-2,482	-2,502	-2,540	-2,556	-2,587	-2,606	-2,609	-9,473	-22,371
Streamline Conservation Programs	-136	-189	-483	-876	-1,291	-1,689	-2,017	-2,121	-2,120	-2,120	-2,975	-13,042
Eliminate Lower Priority Farm Bill Programs	-54	-112	-94	-98	-100	-100	-100	-100	-100	-100	-458	-958
Cap Crop Insurance Companies' Underwriting Gains	0	0	0	-413	-420	-423	-426	-430	-437	-439	-833	-2,988
Eliminate Farm Payment Limit Loopholes	-149	-143	-141	-137	-135	-132	-130	-128	-127	-126	-705	-1,348
Eliminate Livestock Forage Program	-416	-421	-434	-444	-451	-456	-460	-462	-468	-471	-2,166	-4,483
Total	-869	-3,241	-3,610	-4,652	-5,094	-5,537	-5,884	-6,022	-6,058	-6,072	-17,466	-47,039

Note: In addition to the 10-year savings of $47,039 million shown above, $1,660 million in 10-year savings is described separately under the "Eliminate Food for Progress Food Aid Program" proposal for total Farm Bill savings of $48,699 million.

Justification

The Budget proposes to eliminate premium subsidies, commodity payments, and conservation program eligibility for farmers with Adjusted Gross Incomes over $500,000. It is hard to justify to hardworking taxpayers why the Government should provide assistance to wealthy farmers with incomes over $500,000. Doing so undermines the credibility and purpose of farm programs. In 2013 (a year of record-high farm income), only 2.1 percent of farmers had AGIs in excess of this amount.

The Budget proposes to tighten payment limits for farmers and eliminate payment limit loopholes. There is no need for any one producer to receive more than $125,000 in commodity support payments per year ($250,000 for married couples), or for peanut producers-- who already benefit from higher price supports than most producers[1] -- to get special treatment so they are eligible for $250,000 in payments ($500,000 for married couples) if they produce other crops.

The Budget proposes to limit crop insurance premium subsidies. The subsidy the Government currently provides farmers averages 62 percent of their crop insurance premiums; the premium reduction proposal would bring the average premium subsidy down to a more reasonable 48 percent. According to the Government Accountability Office, data shows that the impact on a farmer's average per-acre production costs would be limited to between 1 and 2 percent depending on the crop. Moreover, row crops such as corn, cotton, wheat and soybeans, make up the majority of the liability in the crop insurance program, and those farmers are also eligible for commodity payments. In addition, the Budget proposes to reduce subsidies to the crop insurance companies by setting a 12 percent cap in law for underwriting gains, which is considered a reasonable rate of return for the industry.

The Budget proposes to maximize the efficient use of conservation program funding by prioritizing funding for those programs that have shown positive outcomes and eliminating funding for those programs with limited outcomes. A 2016 Department of Agriculture (USDA) Office of Inspector General (OIG) report found that over 30 percent of Conservation Stewardship Program (CSP) contracts reviewed as part of an audit contained errors or inconsistencies. The errors were due to "ineligible participants receiving CSP contracts and eligible participants receiving excessive program payments."[2] These indicators demonstrate that CSP funding is not always spent in the taxpayers' best interest. In addition, the Budget proposes to eliminate funding for the Regional Conservation Partnership Program, instead favoring legislative flexibility to achieve program goals.

Further, the Budget proposes to eliminate programs for which there is no Federal purpose. The Government should not be singling out select commodities for special assistance (cotton and wool), particularly with a poorly designed program (Economic Adjustment Assistance for Upland Cotton Users)[3], or providing mandatory feed assistance for livestock when producers could purchase subsidized pasture, rangeland, forage insurance to protect against feed losses from drought.

Citations

[1] Congressional Research Service: *Farm Safety-Net Payments Under the 2014 Farm Bill: Comparisons by Program Crop*, Report R44914, (August 2017).

[2] USDA Office of Inspector General: *Controls Over the Conservation Stewardship Program*, Audit Report 10601-0001-32, (September 2016).

[3] USDA Office of Inspector General: *Economic Adjustment Assistance to Users of Upland Cotton*, Audit Report 03601-0002-22, (July 2014).

REFORM THE SUPPLEMENTAL NUTRITION ASSISTANCE PROGRAM
Department of Agriculture

The Budget proposes a suite of legislative proposals for the Supplemental Nutrition Assistance Program (SNAP) encouraging work among able-bodied adults, targeting benefits to the neediest households, and promoting efficiency and integrity in program operations. The Budget would also create a new approach to nutrition assistance that combines traditional SNAP benefits with U.S. Department of Agriculture Foods provided directly to households. This cost-effective approach supports American agriculture, prevents certain types of program abuse, provides state flexibility in delivering food benefits, and ensures the nutritional value of the benefits provided. Combined, these reforms will maintain our commitment to ensuring Americans in need of assistance have access to a nutritious diet while significantly reducing the cost to taxpayers.

Funding Summary
(In millions of dollars)

	2019	2020	2021	2022	2023	2024	2025	2026	2027	2028	2019-23	2019-28
Proposed Change from Current Law............................	-17,169	-18,521	-20,451	-20,468	-21,615	-22,213	-22,353	-23,686	-23,893	-23,157	-98,224	-213,526

Justification

SNAP currently provides low-income households with electronic benefits they can use to buy groceries at authorized retailers. As a primary component of the social safety net, SNAP has grown significantly in the past decade. As expected, SNAP participation grew to historic levels during the recession. However, despite significant economic improvement and a strong recovery in the job market, enrollment in SNAP remains stubbornly high.

The Budget proposes a bold new approach to administering SNAP that combines traditional SNAP benefits with nutritious and 100 percent American grown food provided directly to households. Under the proposal, households receiving $90 or more per month in SNAP benefits will receive a portion of their benefits in the form of a USDA Foods package, which would include items such as shelf-stable milk, ready to eat cereals, pasta, peanut butter, beans and canned fruit, vegetables, and meat, poultry or fish. The remainder of their benefit would go on the SNAP Electronic Benefit Transfer (EBT) card for use at approved grocery retailers. This cost-effective approach will generate significant savings to taxpayers with no loss in food benefits to participants. It will also improve the nutritional value of the benefit provided and reduce the potential for EBT fraud. States will have substantial flexibility in designing the food box delivery system through existing infrastructure, partnerships, or commercial/retail delivery services.

The Budget would also expand on previous reforms aimed at strengthening the expectation for work among able-bodied adults and preserving the benefits for those most in need. This will be achieved by closing eligibility loopholes and limiting categorical eligibility to participants receiving cash benefits from TANF or SSI; modifying income and benefit calculations to ensure benefits are targeted to the neediest households; aligning working age definitions with other Federal programs; eliminating certain exemptions and limiting the use of waivers that rob too many able-bodied adults from the dignity of work. The proposal would motivate states to maximize SNAP administrative efficiencies and to invest in outcome-based employment strategies for SNAP participants. The proposal would also improve program integrity through state accountability and data sharing.

LEASE SHARED SECONDARY LICENSES
Department of Commerce

To promote efficient use of the electromagnetic spectrum, the Administration proposes to authorize the Department of Commerce to negotiate leases with private entities that would expand their access to federal spectrum. This authority will complement ongoing efforts to make Federal spectrum available for commercial uses through auctions conducted by the Federal Communications Commission.

Funding Summary
(In millions of dollars)

	2019	2020	2021	2022	2023	2024	2025	2026	2027	2028	2019-23	2019-28
Proposed Change from Current Law..........................	-50	-55	-55	-60	-65	-70	-70	-80	-80	-85	-285	-670

Justification

Under this proposal, the National Telecommunications and Information Administration (NTIA) would be granted authority to lease access to federal spectrum for commercial use on a non-interference basis, with federal primary users. Working with other federal agencies, NTIA would negotiate sharing arrangements on behalf of the Federal Government and would seek to increase the efficiency of spectrum when possible without causing harmful interference to Federal users authorized to operate in the negotiated bands. In addition to Federal spectrum auctions, leases will provide another option for maximizing the economic value of this scarce spectrum resource. Significant resources will be required by NTIA and other Federal agencies to negotiate and manage these spectrum leases. The cost of administering the program would be offset by a portion of the lease revenue. Therefore the proposal is conservatively estimated to generate approximately $700 million in net deficit reduction for taxpayers.

CREATE SINGLE INCOME-DRIVEN REPAYMENT PLAN
Department of Education

The Budget proposes to simplify student loan repayment by consolidating multiple Income-Driven Repayment (IDR) plans into a single plan. This proposal reduces inefficiencies in the student loan program by establishing several reforms to guarantee that all borrowers in IDR pay an equitable share of their income, and for undergraduate borrowers, reduce the time until loans are forgiven.

Funding Summary
(In millions of dollars)

	2019	2020	2021	2022	2023	2024	2025	2026	2027	2028	2019-23	2019-28
Proposed Change from Current Law..........................	-2,429	-6,006	-9,365	-11,883	-13,885	-15,458	-16,317	-17,228	-17,695	-18,099	-43,568	-128,365

Justification

In recent years, IDR plans, which offer student borrowers the option of making affordable monthly payments based on factors such as income and family size, have grown in popularity. However, the numerous IDR plans currently offered to borrowers overly complicate choosing and enrolling in the right plan. To simplify student loan repayment, the Budget proposes a single IDR plan that provides a pathway to debt relief for struggling borrowers. All new borrowers would pay 12.5 percent of their discretionary income. For borrowers with undergraduate student debt only, any balance remaining after 15 years of repayment would be forgiven. For borrowers with any graduate debt, any balance remaining after 30 years of repayment would be forgiven. To support this ambitious proposal, the Budget proposes a package of targeted reforms to reduce significant inefficiencies in the program. The single IDR plan would remove the standard repayment cap to guarantee that high-income, high-balance borrowers pay an equitable share before their remaining balances are forgiven. In addition, the proposed plan would calculate payments for married borrowers filing separately using their combined household Adjusted Gross Income.

ELIMINATE ACCOUNT MAINTENANCE FEE PAYMENTS TO GUARANTY AGENCIES
Department of Education

The Budget proposes to eliminate unnecessary fee payments to guaranty agencies.

Funding Summary
(In millions of dollars)

	2019	2020	2021	2022	2023	2024	2025	2026	2027	2028	2019-23	2019-28
Proposed Change from Current Law..........................	-656	0	0	0	0	0	0	0	0	0	-656	-656

Justification

Despite dwindling business activities since the move to direct student lending, guaranty agencies from the legacy Federal Family Education Loan (FFEL) Program continue to get paid account maintenance fees. Given the significantly pared back services provided by guaranty agencies, and their ability to generate significant fee income through debt collection activities, the Budget proposes to discontinue these payments.

ELIMINATE PUBLIC SERVICE LOAN FORGIVENESS
Department of Education

The Budget proposes to eliminate the Public Service Loan Forgiveness (PSLF) program and focus assistance on needy undergraduate student borrowers from all professions.

Funding Summary
(In millions of dollars)

	2019	2020	2021	2022	2023	2024	2025	2026	2027	2028	2019-23	2019-28
Proposed Change from Current Law............................	-1,720	-2,979	-3,873	-4,411	-4,851	-5,303	-5,511	-5,597	-5,758	-5,859	-17,834	-45,862

Justification

To support the proposal for a single Income-Driven Repayment (IDR) plan, the Budget proposes a package of targeted student loan reforms and program eliminations, including the elimination of PSLF. PSLF unfairly favors some career choices over others and is complicated for borrowers to navigate. This package would simplify repayment for all new undergraduate borrowers regardless of occupation and create a pathway for expedited debt forgiveness after 15 years of payments instead of after 20 years under current law. PSLF is part of a complex array of Federal aid programs that could benefit from the simplification of aid to needy students. The Budget continues to fully fund Pell Grants to help low-income students afford college, and expands Pell eligibility to high-quality short-term programs, enabling students to obtain the skills they need for today's workforce more quickly than the traditional two or four-year degree.

ELIMINATE SUBSIDIZED STUDENT LOANS
Department of Education

The Budget proposes to eliminate inefficient interest subsidies for certain undergraduate loans and focus resources on more effective forms of support for needy undergraduate students.

Funding Summary
(In millions of dollars)

	2019	2020	2021	2022	2023	2024	2025	2026	2027	2028	2019-23	2019-28
Proposed Change from Current Law............	-1,500	-2,580	-2,886	-2,973	-2,992	-3,008	-3,050	-3,096	-3,216	-3,254	-12,931	-28,555

Justification

To support the proposal for a single Income-Driven Repayment (IDR) plan, the Budget proposes a package of targeted reforms and program eliminations, including the elimination of subsidized loans. Under current law, the Government pays interest on subsidized loans for eligible low- and middle-income undergraduates while the student is in school or deferment. While the in-school interest subsidy has not been rigorously evaluated, lessons from behavioral economics indicate that the subsidy is less likely to increase postsecondary enrollment, due to the complexity of the interest rate benefit, than straightforward need-based grants to students. The subsidy is also poorly targeted as it is provided to borrowers with low pre-enrollment income but does not consider the income of borrowers during repayment. Borrowers with unaffordable debt burdens relative to their income during repayment can manage their debt through income-driven repayment and ultimately receive forgiveness. Subsidized loans are part of a complex array of Federal aid programs that could benefit from the simplification of aid to needy students.

DIVEST THE POWER MARKETING ADMINISTRATIONS' TRANSMISSION ASSETS
Department of Energy

The Budget proposes to sell the transmission assets of the Department of Energy's Power Marketing Administrations (PMAs), which include Southwestern Power Administration (SWPA), Western Area Power Administration (WAPA), and Bonneville Power Administration (BPA). The private sector is best suited to own and operate electricity transmission assets. Eliminating or reducing the Federal Government's role in owning and operating transmission assets and increasing the private sector's role encourages a more efficient allocation of economic resources and mitigates unnecessary risk to taxpayers.

Funding Summary
(In millions of dollars)

	2019	2020	2021	2022	2023	2024	2025	2026	2027	2028	2019-23	2019-28
Divest WAPA Transmission Assets......	0	-580	0	0	0	0	0	0	0	0	-580	-580
Divest SWPA Transmission Assets......	0	-15	0	0	0	0	0	0	0	0	-15	-15
Divest BPA Transmission Assets......	0	-1,733	-488	-483	-493	-452	-386	-386	-386	-386	-3,197	-5,193
Total......	0	-2,328	-488	-483	-493	-452	-386	-386	-386	-386	-3,792	-5,788

Justification

The Budget proposes to sell the electricity transmission assets currently owned by the Southwestern Power Administration, the Western Area Power Administration, and the Bonneville Power Administration. Divestiture of Federal assets can encourage private capital investment in the Nation's infrastructure and relieve long-term pressure on the deficit related to future capital investments. The vast majority of the Nation's electricity infrastructure is owned and operated by for-profit investor owned utilities. Ownership of transmission assets is best carried out by the private sector where there are appropriate market and regulatory incentives.

REFORM THE LAWS GOVERNING HOW THE POWER MARKETING ADMINISTRATIONS ESTABLISH POWER RATES
Department of Energy

The Budget proposes to change the statutory requirement that the Power Marketing Administrations' power rates be limited to recovering costs to a structure that considers appropriate market incentives. A market based approach for establishing rates for power sales from Federal dams encourages a more efficient allocation of economic resources.

Funding Summary
(In millions of dollars)

	2019	2020	2021	2022	2023	2024	2025	2026	2027	2028	2019-23	2019-28
Proposed Change from Current Law............................	-162	-169	-173	-182	-188	-192	-199	-206	-211	-217	-874	-1,899

Justification

The Power Marketing Administrations (PMAs) sell wholesale electricity generated at multipurpose dams owned and operated by the Army Corps of Engineers and the Bureau of Reclamation. Current law requires the PMAs to generate revenues by establishing rates charged to utility customers to recover all costs, including annual operating and maintenance costs and the taxpayers' investment in the power portions of dams and in transmission lines, and permits the PMAs to defer repayment of prior capital investment by the taxpayers. By contrast, the vast majority of the Nation's electricity needs are met through for-profit investor owned utilities, which are subject to State and/or Federal regulatory oversight in the establishment of rates. Eliminating the requirement that PMA rates be limited to a cost-based structure and requiring instead that these rates be based on consideration of appropriate market incentives, including whether they are just and reasonable, would encourage a more efficient allocation of economic resources and could result in faster recoupment of taxpayer investments.

REPEAL BORROWING AUTHORITY FOR WESTERN AREA POWER ADMINISTRATION
Department of Energy

The Budget proposes to repeal Western Area Power Administration's (WAPA) authority to borrow up to $3.25 billion in emergency funds authorized by the American Recovery and Reinvestment Act of 2009 (Recovery Act) for the purpose of constructing and/or funding projects within WAPA's service territory that deliver, or facilitate the delivery of, power generated by renewable energy resources. Repealing this authority encourages a more efficient allocation of economic resources and mitigates unnecessary risk to taxpayers.

Funding Summary
(In millions of dollars)

	2019	2020	2021	2022	2023	2024	2025	2026	2027	2028	2019-23	2019-28
Proposed Change from Current Law............................	-450	-875	-75	575	275	110	-50	-50	-50	-50	-550	-640

Justification

The vast majority of the Nation's electricity needs are met through for-profit investor-owned utilities. Investments in transmission assets are best carried out by the private sector where there are appropriate market and regulatory incentives. Federal financing of transmission assets places unnecessary risk on taxpayers and results in an inefficient allocation of economic resources. Further, activities under the Recovery Act, which was enacted in response to the 2009 Great Recession, are no longer needed. Since its inception, the program has made less than $300 million in total loans to three transmission projects. As of fiscal year-end 2017, the program held less than $100 million in outstanding loan balances owed to the Department of the Treasury.

ELIMINATE THE SOCIAL SERVICES BLOCK GRANT
Department of Health and Human Services

The Budget proposes to eliminate the Social Services Block Grant (SSBG) because it lacks strong performance measures, is not well targeted, and is not a core function of the Federal Government. States do not have to demonstrate that they are using funds effectively in order to continue receiving funding. In addition, SSBG funds services that are also funded through other Federal programs, such as early childhood education services funded through Head Start and child welfare services funded by Title IV-E programs.

Funding Summary
(In millions of dollars)

	2019	2020	2021	2022	2023	2024	2025	2026	2027	2028	2019-23	2019-28
Proposed Change from Current Law..........................	-1,411	-1,649	-1,700	-1,700	-1,700	-1,700	-1,700	-1,700	-1,700	-1,700	-8,160	-16,660

Justification

SSBG is a permanently authorized program, which funds a wide variety of services. Examples of services include child care, child and adult protective services, foster care, and special services for the disabled. Overall, there are 29 broad service categories within SSBG (including "other"). However, better targeted State and Federal programs currently fund most of these services. SSBG lacks strong performance metrics and the means to hold States accountable for spending SSBG funds effectively.

MEDICAID: ADDRESS WASTEFUL SPENDING, FRAUD, AND ABUSE
Department of Health and Human Services

The Budget proposes to provide new authorities to States and HHS to improve Medicaid integrity and reduce wasteful spending by ensuring providers who engage in fraudulent or abusive activities do not enroll in Medicaid, improving Medicaid payment and billing policies to prevent wasteful spending, increasing safeguards for patients receiving care in home- and community-based settings, and continuing the Medicaid Disproportionate Share Hospital (DSH) payment reductions.

Funding Summary
(In millions of dollars)

	2019	2020	2021	2022	2023	2024	2025	2026	2027	2028	2019-23	2019-28
Continue Medicaid Disproportionate Share Hospital (DSH) Allotment Reductions............	0	0	0	0	0	0	0	-6,510	-6,490	-6,470	0	-19,470
Consolidate Provider Enrollment Screening for Medicare, Medicaid, and CHIP..................	0	0	0	0	0	0	0	0	0	0	0	0
Streamline the Medicaid Terminations Process............	0	0	0	0	0	0	0	0	0	0	0	0
Total......................................	0	0	0	0	0	0	0	-6,510	-6,490	-6,470	0	-19,470

Note: In addition to the above proposals, the Budget also proposes the following reforms: 1) Implement Prepayment Controls to Prevent Inappropriate Personal Care Services Payments; 2) Expand Medicaid Fraud Control Unit Review to Additional Care Settings; and 3) Prohibit Medicaid Payments to Public Providers in Excess of Costs. Estimates for these reforms were not available at the time of Budget publication.

Justification

Ensuring Medicaid program integrity requires coordination among States and the Federal Government. States have primary responsibility for combating Medicaid fraud, waste, and abuse, while the Federal Government provides States guidance and technical support to detect, deter, and monitor fraud and abuse, as well as take action against those that commit or participate in fraudulent activities.

States can limit improper payments and expensive "pay and chase" activities by preventing fraudulent providers from enrolling in Medicaid, but not all States conduct the comprehensive screening activities required by law. Consistent with recommendations from the HHS Office of Inspector General (OIG), the Budget proposes to centralize the screening of all Medicaid, Medicare, and Children's Health Insurance (CHIP) providers.[1] Making the Federal Government the single source for screening would reduce duplication and ensure bad actors cannot move between the programs. The Budget also proposes strengthening requirements for terminating Medicaid providers and sharing termination information among the States.

To the extent fee-for-service Medicaid rates to certain facilities result in aggregate provider payments that are lower than what Medicare would have paid for comparable services, States may make supplemental payments to such providers. The Government Accountability Office has raised concerns about the transparency and oversight of supplemental payments, citing a lack of timely information to determine whether payments meet statutory requirements, and instances of payments to hospitals that greatly exceeded costs. To improve fiscal integrity and transparency in Medicaid payment policy, the Budget previews guidance from HHS to improve timely and complete data collection on Medicaid supplemental payments, including the financing of such payments, and proposes to limit reimbursement to Government providers to no more than the cost of providing services to Medicaid beneficiaries.

The Budget proposes to reduce duplicative spending by continuing the Medicaid Disproportionate Share (DSH) hospital allotment reductions since the new Market-Based Health Care Block Grants proposed in the Budget provide States with resources to maintain coverage for those previously covered by Obamacare.

In addition, many elderly and disabled Medicaid beneficiaries rely on personal care services (PCS) to get needed care in their communities and maintain their independence. The increasing volume of fraud involving PCS is a top concern of HHS and State Medicaid Fraud Control Units. Consistent with an OIG recommendation, the Budget previews guidance to assign PCS attendants unique identifiers that would be listed on claims along with the specific dates that they performed services. Further, given evidence that States' unsuccessful prepayment edits contributed to improper payments, the Budget proposes to implement claims edits to automatically deny unusual PCS payments, as well as extend States' authority to investigate and prosecute abuse or neglect cases in home- and community-based care settings.[2,3]

Citations

[1] HHS Office of Inspector General: *Medicaid Enhanced Provider Enrollment Screenings Have Not Been Fully Implemented,* OEI-05-13-00520, (May 2016).

[2] HHS Office of Inspector General: *Personal Care Services: Trends, Vulnerabilities, and Recommendations for Improvement,* OIG-12-12-01, (November 2012).

[3] HHS Office of Inspector General: *Payments Made in Error for Personal Care Services During Institutional Stays,* OEI-07-06-00620, (August 2008).

MEDICAID: DRUG PRICING AND PAYMENT IMPROVEMENTS
Department of Health and Human Services

The Budget proposes new Medicaid demonstration authority for up to five States to test drug coverage and financing reforms that build on private sector best practices. The Budget also proposes changes to clarify definitions under the Medicaid Drug Rebate Program to prevent manufacturers from claiming inappropriately low rebates.

Funding Summary
(In millions of dollars)

	2019	2020	2021	2022	2023	2024	2025	2026	2027	2028	2019-23	2019-28
Test allowing State Medicaid programs to negotiate prices directly with drug manufacturers and set formulary for coverage............	0	-5	-10	-10	-10	-10	-10	-10	-10	-10	-35	-85
Clarify definitions under the Medicaid Drug Rebate Program to prevent inappropriately low manufacturer rebates.............	-26	-26	-26	-26	-31	-31	-37	-37	-37	-42	-135	-319
Total.......................................	-26	-31	-36	-36	-41	-41	-47	-47	-47	-52	-170	-404

Justification

While outpatient prescription drugs is an optional Medicaid benefit, all State Medicaid programs currently cover prescriptions drugs through the Medicaid Drug Rebate Program. Per capita Medicaid spending on prescription drugs increased by an average of 7.5 percent per year from 2013 through 2016 (reflecting total Federal and State spending net of rebates). A primary driver of these spending increases which strain State budgets and burden taxpayers was the introduction of new, high cost drugs for various conditions. For example, data from the Centers for Medicare and Medicaid Services (CMS) indicate that State Medicaid programs spent more than $2.8 billion in 2015 on a new class of hepatitis C treatments.

Under the Medicaid Drug Rebate Program, States who include optional drug benefits are required to cover any prescription drug offered by manufacturers who have entered into statutorily defined rebate agreements with the Department of Health and Human Services (HHS). This decades-old statutory structure hampers State-led innovation, since States are unable to make formulary decisions to meet the needs of their populations or control the total cost of their Medicaid drug benefit.

Under the Medicaid prescription drug demonstration proposed in the Budget, participating States would determine their own drug formularies, coupled with an appeals process to protect beneficiary access to non-covered drugs based on medical need, and negotiate drug prices directly with manufacturers, instead of participating in the statutory drug rebate program. The proposal includes exempting prices negotiated under the demonstration from Medicaid's Best Price reporting requirements, facilitating price negotiation between States and manufacturers. HHS and participating States would rigorously evaluate these demonstrations, which would provide States with new tools to control drug costs and tailor drug coverage decisions to State needs.

Separately, the Budget proposes a legislative change to clarify the Medicaid definition of brand drugs, which would address inappropriate interpretations leading manufacturers to classify certain brand and over the counter drugs as generics for Medicaid rebate purposes, reducing rebate amounts owed.

MEDICAID: STRENGTHEN OPERATIONS AND INCREASE STATE FLEXIBILITY
Department of Health and Human Services

In addition to the Medicaid program flexibilities included in the Budget proposal to repeal and replace Obamacare, the Budget proposes to empower States to further modernize Medicaid benefits and target eligibility. In determining Medicaid eligibility, the Budget would enable States to consider savings and other assets, count lottery winnings as income, and ensure Federal funds are only available for individuals with verified immigration status. In addition, the Budget would allow States to increase co-payments for non-emergency use of the emergency department. These proposals empower the Federal and State governments to be partners in greater fiscal responsibility, preserving and protecting the Medicaid program for Americans who truly need it.

Funding Summary
(In millions of dollars)

	2019	2020	2021	2022	2023	2024	2025	2026	2027	2028	2019-23	2019-28
Allow States to Apply Asset Tests to Modified Adjusted Gross Income Standard Populations...............	-50	-100	-190	-200	-220	-230	-240	-260	-270	-290	-760	-2,050
Reduce Maximum Allowable Home Equity for Medicaid Eligibility..................	0	0	0	0	0	0	0	0	0	0	0	0
Require Documentation of Satisfactory Immigration Status Before Receipt of Medicaid Benefits..............	-170	-180	-190	-200	-210	-220	-230	-250	-260	-280	-950	-2,190
Increase Limit on Medicaid Co-payments for Nonemergency Use of Emergency Department........	-60	-110	-110	-120	-130	-140	-140	-150	-160	-170	-530	-1,290
Define Lottery Winnings and Other Lump-Sum Payments as Income for Purpose of Medicaid Eligibility...............	-3	-3	-4	-5	-5	-5	-6	-6	-6	-7	-20	-50
Total......................	-283	-393	-494	-525	-565	-595	-616	-666	-696	-747	-2,260	-5,580

Justification

The current Federal framework for Medicaid fails to provide States with the flexibility to design their Medicaid programs to meet the unique needs of their State. At the same time, Medicaid spending is increasing at an unsustainable rate, and it is critical that benefits be targeted to the most vulnerable populations. The Administration believes States, not the Federal Government, are in the best position to assess the needs of their Medicaid population, target benefits to those most in need, and implement innovative reforms. The Budget would grant States additional flexibility in designing their Medicaid programs and make them more efficient by providing options to increase co-pays for improper use of the emergency department and modify eligibility requirements to ensure the safety net is reserved for the most vulnerable populations.

The Budget would enable States to focus on the most vulnerable populations. By allowing States to consider savings, lottery winnings, and other assets in determining Medicaid eligibility, the Budget would focus Medicaid spending on individuals who do not have significant assets. The Budget also proposes to not pay for medical assistance of individuals who have not verified their immigration status, and thus their eligibility for Medicaid.

By allowing States to increase co-payments for non-emergency use of the emergency department, the Budget would encourage beneficiaries to engage in personal financial responsibility and proper use of healthcare resources. Medicaid beneficiaries use the emergency department at an almost two-fold higher rate than the privately insured.[1,2] "Super-utilizers", who have four or more emergency department visits per year, comprise 4.5 to 8 percent of all emergency department patients across payers but account for 21 to 28 percent of all visits.[3] The Centers for Medicare and Medicaid Services (CMS) has already granted waivers to several States to increase co-payments for non-emergency use of the emergency department. The Budget would allow States to pursue this flexibility without going through the waiver process.

Citations

[1] Garcia et al.: *Emergency Department Visitors and Visits: Who Used the Emergency Room in 2007?* CDC, NCHS Data Brief No 38, (2010).

[2] Mann, Cindy: *Reducing Nonurgent Use of Emergency Departments and Improving Appropriate Care in Appropriate Settings,* CMCS Informational Bulletin, www.medicaid.gov/Federal-Policy-Guidance/Downloads/CIB-01-16-14.pdf, (January 2014).

[3] LaCalle et al.: *Frequent users of emergency departments: The myths, the data and the policy implications,* Annals of Emergency Medicine, 56:42-48, (2010).

MEDICARE AND MEDICAID: INCREASE OVERSIGHT OF OPIOID PRESCRIPTIONS AND EXPAND TREATMENT OPTIONS

Department of Health and Human Services

To address the opioid epidemic, for Medicaid, the Budget proposes expanding coverage of comprehensive and evidence-based Medication Assisted Treatment (MAT) options, previews forthcoming guidance from the Centers for Medicare and Medicaid Services (CMS) that will set minimum standards for State Drug Utilization Reviews (DUR) to reduce clinical abuse, and requires States to track and act on high prescribers and utilizers of prescription drugs. For Medicare, the Budget proposes to prevent prescription drug abuse and to provide comprehensive substance abuse treatment.

Funding Summary
(In millions of dollars)

	2019	2020	2021	2022	2023	2024	2025	2026	2027	2028	2019-23	2019-28
Require plan participation in a program to prevent prescription drug abuse in Medicare Part D..........	-10	-10	-10	-10	-10	-10	-10	-10	-10	-10	-50	-100
Require coverage of all MAT options in Medicaid............	35	25	-20	-75	-110	-130	-135	-145	-150	-160	-145	-865
Total Savings.......................	25	15	-30	-85	-120	-140	-145	-155	-160	-170	-195	-965

Note: In addition to the above proposals, the Budget also proposes the following reforms: 1) Prevent abusive prescribing by establishing HHS reciprocity with the Drug Enforcement Administration to terminate provider prescribing authority; 2) Provide comprehensive coverage of substance abuse treatment in Medicare; and 3) Track high prescribers and utilizers of prescription drugs in Medicaid. Estimates for these reforms were not available at the time of Budget publication.

Justification

Rates of drug overdose deaths have continued to increase rapidly over the past 15 years, and the rise in prescription and illicit opioid abuse has been the primary driver of this increase. In 2015, the rate of drug overdose deaths was more than 2.5 times the rate in 1999 with deaths from heroin overdoses triple the rate in 2010, and more recently, an influx of illicitly made fentanyl and fentanyl analogs has fueled a substantial increase in synthetic opioid overdose deaths. Despite the fact that there are effective evidence-based treatments for Opioid Use Disorder (OUD), only about 32 percent of Medicaid beneficiaries with OUD received treatment in 2015.

Therefore, the Budget includes a series of proposals to enhance oversight of opioid prescriptions in Medicaid and increase treatment options. While all State Medicaid programs currently cover some MATs for OUD, many States exclude certain treatment options. For example 17 States currently exclude methadone maintenance treatment. The Budget proposes a legislative change requiring that State Medicaid programs cover all Food and Drug Administration-approved MAT options. These up-front investments in expanded MAT treatment are expected to reduce total Medicaid expenditures over time as more individuals recover from OUD. In addition, the Medicaid statute requires that each State develop a DUR program targeted in part at reducing clinical abuse/misuse, but States vary greatly in the standards they set. CMS, working in partnership with States, stakeholders, and medical experts, will develop and issue guidance to States on the minimum standards they must meet for DUR programs to reduce OUD. The Budget proposes new legislative authority requiring States to track high prescribers and utilizers of prescription drugs in Medicaid, such as through a Prescription Drug Monitoring Program. This proposal would ensure that all States meet high standards of oversight for opioid prescriptions.

The Comprehensive Addiction Recovery Act (CARA) of 2016 directed CMS to propose a framework under which Medicare Part D plan sponsors may establish a drug management program for beneficiaries at risk for prescription drug abuse or misuse and require those determined to be at risk to obtain opioid prescriptions from specific providers and pharmacies, preventing the ability to seek opioids from multiple providers and pharmacies. In accordance with the President's initiatives on combatting the drug abuse and opioid overdose epidemic, the Budget proposes to strengthen the provisions specified in CARA by providing the Secretary of Health and Human Services (HHS) with authority to establish a mandatory prescriber and/or pharmacy "lock-in" program in Medicare Part D in which all Part D plans would be required to participate.

In addition, for Medicare, the Budget proposes to test and expand nationwide a bundled payment for community-based MAT, including Medicare reimbursement for methadone treatment for the first time. In addition, the Budget proposes to authorize the Secretary of HHS to work with the Drug Enforcement Administration to revoke a provider's certificate (which allows a provider to prescribe controlled substances) when that provider is barred from billing Medicare based on a pattern of abusive prescribing. Cutting off Medicare funding for abusive prescription practices not only helps bring premiums down for seniors, it promotes sound public health policy.

MEDICARE: ADDRESS FRAUD AND ABUSE
Department of Health and Human Services

The Budget proposes to strengthen the tools and authorities the Medicare program has to detect and prevent Medicare fraud and abuse and to take action against individuals who look to defraud the Medicare program and harm beneficiaries in the process. Specifically, the Budget proposes to improve Medicare prescription drug reporting and payment accuracy. In addition, the Budget proposes to strengthen the provider enrollment process and the Medicare program's authorities to remove fraudulent and abusive providers from the program.

Funding Summary
(In millions of dollars)

	2019	2020	2021	2022	2023	2024	2025	2026	2027	2028	2019-23	2019-28
Suspend coverage and payment for questionable Part D prescriptions and incomplete clinical information...............	-30	-30	-40	-40	-50	-40	-40	-50	-50	-50	-190	-420
Prevent abuse of Medicare coverage when another source has primary responsibility for prescription drug coverage....................	-10	-30	-30	-30	-40	-40	-50	-50	-60	-70	-140	-410
Prevent fraud by enforcing reporting of enrollment changes through civil monetary penalties for providers and suppliers who fail to update enrollment records......................	-2	-2	-3	-3	-3	-3	-4	-4	-4	-4	-13	-32
Allow revocation and denial of provider enrollment based on affiliation with sanctioned entity.......................	0	0	-6	-6	-6	-6	-6	-6	-6	-11	-18	-53
Require clearinghouses and billing agents acting on behalf of Medicare providers and suppliers to enroll in the program...................	0	0	0	0	0	0	0	0	0	0	0	0
Ensure providers that violate Medicare's safety requirements and have harmed patients cannot quickly reenter the program..................	0	0	0	0	0	0	0	0	0	0	0	0
Assess a penalty on physicians and practitioners who order services or supplies without proper documentation..................	0	0	0	0	0	0	0	0	0	0	0	0
Clarify authority for the Healthcare Fraud Prevention Partnership....................	0	0	0	0	0	0	0	0	0	0	0	0
Alter Open Payments reporting and publication cycle............	0	0	0	0	0	0	0	0	0	0	0	0
Publish the National Provider Identifier for covered recipients in the Open Payments Program...................	0	0	0	0	0	0	0	0	0	0	0	0
Improve safety and quality of care by requiring accreditation organizations to publicly report Medicare survey and certification reports...............	0	0	0	0	0	0	0	0	0	0	0	0
Total......................	-42	-62	-79	-79	-99	-89	-100	-110	-120	-135	-361	-915

Note: In addition to the above proposals, the Budget also proposes to expand prior authorization to additional Medicare fee-for-service items at high risk of fraud, waste, and abuse. Estimates for this reform were not available at the time of Budget publication.

Justification

The Budget includes two proposals to improve Medicare prescription drug reporting and payment accuracy. Currently, coverage of Part D drugs is limited to medically-accepted indications that are not otherwise covered by Parts A or B. Statute requires that the drug must be dispensed only upon prescription, but does not address situations where a provider may be abusing prescribing privileges, or, despite an approved indication, expert clinical opinion discourages drug use. A 2017 Department of Health and Human Services (HHS) Office of Inspector General (OIG) report noted that 90,000 beneficiaries were at serious risk of opioid misuse or overdose, and 400 prescribers had questionable opioid prescribing practices.[1] The Budget would provide the Secretary with additional authority to suspend coverage and payment for drugs that present an imminent risk to patients and when they are prescribed by providers who have been engaged in misprescribing or over prescribing drugs with abuse potential. The Centers for Medicare and Medicaid Services (CMS) would also be given the authority to require additional clinical information as a condition of coverage.

Additionally, insurers and third party administrators of group health plans are required to report hospital and medical coverage for Medicare beneficiaries that is primary to Medicare; however, there is not a comparable requirement for prescription drug coverage. The Budget would extend this requirement to include drug coverage and ensure Medicare does not cover drugs where another insurer has financial responsibility.

The Budget also includes several additional proposals that would further address fraud and abuse in Medicare.

Expand prior authorization to additional Medicare fee-for-service items at high risk of fraud, waste, and abuse—The Budget proposes to expand the Medicare program's authority to conduct prior authorization on certain items or services that are at high risk of fraud and abuse. CMS has tested prior authorization on a couple of items and services that are common targets for high improper payments, such as power wheel chairs and non-emergency ambulance services. Preliminary evaluation results indicate that prior authorization can be an effective tool for dissuading fraudulent actors and reducing inappropriate utilization. The proposal would reduce improper payments and save taxpayer dollars from paying for Medicare services that are not medically necessary by ensuring that the right payment goes to the right provider for the appropriate service.

Prevent fraud by enforcing reporting of enrollment changes—Currently, providers and suppliers are required to update enrollment records to remain in compliance with the Medicare program. Unreported changes in provider enrollment information leave room for fraud to take place. The Budget proposes to increase CMS' authority to enforce appropriate reporting of changes in provider enrollment information through civil monetary penalties or other intermediate sanctions to mitigate the associated risk.

Allow revocation and denial of provider enrollment based on affiliation with a sanctioned entity—Provider and supplier enrollment is an essential program integrity tool, as it is the gateway to billing the Medicare program and ensuring only those providers and suppliers who are eligible furnish services or items to Medicare beneficiaries. The Budget proposes to strengthen the enrollment process and the Medicare program's authority to remove bad actors from the program.

Currently, the Medicare program cannot revoke a provider's enrollment or deny a provider's billing privileges if the program discovers through its own internal investigations that the provider has a connection to an entity that Medicare previously sanctioned, unless the provider self-discloses the relationship. This creates a loophole where a provider that was previously sanctioned, potentially as a result of abusive billing or fraud, could start a new organization and return to doing business with Medicare. The Budget proposes to close this loophole by providing the Medicare program with the authority to take administrative action against entities that have owners, managing employees, officers, or directors with direct financial and operational affiliation to a previously sanctioned Medicare entity.

Require clearinghouses and billing agents acting on behalf of Medicare providers and suppliers to enroll in the program—This proposal expands provider screening authorities by establishing a registration process for clearinghouses and billing agents that act on behalf of Medicare providers and suppliers. This proposal would also allow CMS to obtain organizational information from clearinghouses and billing agents.

Ensure providers that violate Medicare's safety requirements and have harmed patients cannot quickly reenter the program—This proposal allows the Secretary to enforce an exception to Medicare's reasonable assurance period in cases of patient harm or neglect. The reasonable assurance period currently allows providers and suppliers who have been terminated from participation in Medicare for not complying with Federal requirements to reenter the program after a preliminary showing of compliance, even under circumstances that conflict with Medicare's minimum reenrollment bar, which puts beneficiaries at an increased risk of patient harm. This narrow exception to current practice would only be used in egregious cases of patient harm or patient neglect.

Assess a penalty on physicians and practitioners who order services or supplies without proper documentation—This proposal allows the Secretary to assess an administrative penalty on providers for claims that have not been properly documented for high risk, high cost items or services. The proposal only applies when there is insufficient documentation and would not apply to the determination of whether a fully documented ordered item or service was reasonable and necessary.

Clarify authority for the Healthcare Fraud Prevention Partnership—This proposal establishes explicit authority for the Healthcare Fraud Prevention Partnership and its activities. Currently, the Partnership operates under the authority established for the Health Care Fraud and Abuse Control Program, which allows for data sharing to address fraud and abuse in health insurance. By providing explicit authority, the Partnership would be able to clearly define the rules and responsibilities of its members and expand the scope of allowable activities to address the full spectrum of fraud and abuse in the healthcare sector. These include efforts to examine large public health issues that have fraud, waste, and abuse implications, such as opioid misuse.

Alter the Open Payments reporting and publication cycle—This proposal changes the annual publication date for the Open Payments data from June 30th to October 1st. This change would reduce burden for both industry and providers and improve data accuracy by allowing more time for data submission and review.

Publish the National Provider Identifier for covered recipients in the Open Payments Program—This proposal would allow CMS to publish the National Provider Identifier (NPI) on the Open Payments website, further increasing transparency and making the dataset more robust and useful to users. Open Payments is a Federal program that collects information about the payments or in-kind gifts that drug and device companies make to physicians and teaching hospitals (e.g., travel, research, gifts, speaking fees, and meals). Under current law, CMS cannot publish a manufacturer's or group purchasing organization's NPI along with information about payments or transfer of value.

Improve the safety and quality of care by requiring accreditation organizations to publicly report Medicare survey and certification reports—In order to participate in Medicare, providers must certify that they comply with the Medicare Conditions of Participation (CoPs). CMS grants national accrediting organizations (AOs), such as the Joint Commission, "deeming" authority, meaning that the AO is responsible for accrediting that the provider meets the Medicare CoPs. Providers with "deemed status" are not subject to the Medicare survey and certification process if it has already been surveyed by the AO. Accreditation is voluntary, but nearly 90 percent of hospitals participate in Medicare via accreditation and deemed status. For hospitals without "deemed status," CMS publicly reports survey findings and acceptable plans of correction (PoCs) when a hospital is found to be out of compliance. AOs do not publicly report survey findings for accredited hospitals, and CMS does not have the authority to publish surveys conducted by AOs. This proposal would require AOs to publish survey findings for all hospitals as part of their contract as a deeming authority. This proposal would increase transparency around the quality of hospitals, especially of instances that could pose harm to beneficiaries.

Citations

[1] Health and Human Services Office of Inspector General: *Opioids in Medicare Part D: Concerns about Extreme Use and Questionable Prescribing*, OEI-02-17-00250, (July 2017).

MEDICARE: DRUG PRICING AND PAYMENT IMPROVEMENTS
Department of Health and Human Services

The Budget proposes new strategies to address high drug prices and increase access to lifesaving medicines by rationalizing the current payment incentive structures in Part D and Part B and fostering greater competition.

Funding Summary
(In millions of dollars)

	2019	2020	2021	2022	2023	2024	2025	2026	2027	2028	2019-23	2019-28
Permanently authorize a successful pilot on retroactive Medicare Part D coverage for low-income beneficiaries.......	0	-20	-30	-30	-30	-30	-40	-40	-40	-40	-110	-300
Increase Medicare Part D plan formulary flexibility................	-280	-404	-444	-487	-530	-576	-618	-669	-725	-784	-2,145	-5,517
Eliminate cost-sharing on generic drugs for low-income beneficiaries..........................	-30	-40	-40	-20	-20	-10	-20	-10	-10	-10	-150	-210
Require Medicare Part D plans to apply a substantial portion of rebates at the point of sale.......................	1,785	2,727	3,139	3,533	3,930	4,351	4,801	5,356	5,983	6,555	15,114	42,160
Exclude manufacturer discounts from the calculation of beneficiary out-of-pocket costs in the Medicare Part D coverage gap......................	-1,490	-2,370	-3,360	-4,800	-5,300	-4,740	-5,360	-5,840	-6,330	-7,430	-17,320	-47,020
Establish a beneficiary out-of-pocket maximum in the Medicare Part D catastrophic phase...........................	377	541	592	648	706	767	825	892	966	1,045	2,864	7,359
Reform exclusivity for first generics to spur greater competition and access.........	-118	-130	-142	-169	-169	-165	-194	-209	-225	-267	-728	-1,788
Total..................................	244	304	-285	-1,325	-1,413	-403	-606	-520	-381	-931	-2,475	-5,316

Note: In addition to the above proposals, the Budget also proposes the following reforms: 1) Authorize the HHS Secretary to leverage Medicare Part D plans' negotiating power for certain drugs covered under Part B; 2) Address abusive drug pricing by manufacturers by establishing an inflation limit for reimbursement of Medicare Part B drugs; 3) Improve manufacturers' reporting of average sales prices to set accurate payment rates; 4) Modify payment for drugs hospitals purchase through the 340B discount program and require a minimum level of charity care for hospitals to receive a payment adjustment related to uncompensated care; and 5) Reduce Wholesale Acquisition Cost (WAC)-based payments. Estimates for these reforms were not available at the time of Budget publication.

Justification

Medicare Part D prescription drug spending is projected to total $94 billion in 2017, an increase of 97 percent since 2007.[1] Research has shown that the misaligned incentives in the Part D benefit design help drive this trend by rewarding drug pricing and price concession strategies that encourage plans to provide favorable formulary placement and to promote utilization of high cost drugs when lower cost options are available.[2] This ultimately results in higher spending for both beneficiaries and the Government. In 2015, nearly 1 in 10 Medicare Part D enrollees (3.6 million), including 2.6 million beneficiaries receiving low-income subsidies, reached the highest level of spending in the benefit structure, the catastrophic phase, where Medicare covers 80 percent of costs.[3] On average, enrollees with spending in the catastrophic phase incurred 40 percent of their total out-of-pocket costs above the threshold in 2015.

The Budget would improve the Part D drug benefit, leveraging the knowledge gained over 12 years since its implementation in 2006. The Budget would provide true catastrophic coverage for all beneficiaries through a newly established out-of-pocket maximum. In addition, the Budget eliminates cost sharing for generic drugs for low-income seniors to encourage the use of higher value products, requires plans to share a substantial portion of savings from negotiated rebates with beneficiaries at the pharmacy counter, and enables tougher Part D plan price negotiations with drug manufacturers through increased plan formulary flexibilities. The Budget would also permanently authorize a Medicare Part D demonstration that provides retroactive and point-of-sale (POS) coverage to certain low-income beneficiaries through a single plan. Working through one plan for retroactive coverage establishes a single point of contact for beneficiaries to resolve coverage issues, eliminates incentives that impede reimbursement of retroactive claims, and has proven to be less disruptive to beneficiaries.

Generally, Medicare reimburses Part B drugs provided in doctors' offices or hospitals based on the drugs average sales price (ASP) plus six percent; however, there is no limit to how much Medicare's payment rate for a drug can increase over time, allowing for dramatic price increases. The Medicare Payment Advisory Commission (MedPAC) found evidence that the ASP grows faster than inflation for many high expenditure drugs.[4] Additionally, the Center for Medicare and Medicaid Services relies on manufacturers to submit sales data to calculate ASPs for Part B drugs, but currently not all manufacturers are required to report this data. When payment rates are based on incomplete ASP data, Medicare's payment rate does not accurately reflect price concessions and other factors that would ensure accurate payment. To address these issues, the Budget would require all Part B drug manufacturers to report ASP data and provide the Secretary with the authority to apply penalties to manufacturers who do not report required data. The Budget would place a limit on increases in Medicare's ASP-based payment for a drug based on inflation as measured by the consumer price index. Additionally, the Budget proposes to modify hospitals' payment for drugs acquired through the 340B drug discount program to reward them based on the charity care they provide and to reduce payment if they provide little to no charity care. Finally, the Budget would provide the Secretary of Health and Human Services with authority to consolidate certain drugs currently covered under Part B into Part D where there are savings to be gained through increased price competition.

When ASP data are not available, Medicare largely reimburses new, single-source Part B drugs at 106 percent of wholesale acquisition cost (WAC). Unlike an ASP, a drug's WAC does not incorporate prompt-pay or other discounts benefitting the manufacturer. If discounts are available on these new Part B drugs, Medicare is paying more than it otherwise would under the ASP-based formula. MedPAC found evidence that Medicare payments do not reflect discounts available when drugs were priced based on WAC.[4] To reduce excessive payments, the Budget would reduce the payment rate for drugs currently paid at 106 percent of WAC to 103 percent of WAC.

The Budget proposes to give the Food and Drug Administration greater ability to bring generics to market faster by incentivizing more competition among generic manufacturers. This proposal would result in substantial savings to Medicare. The Budget proposes to ensure that first-to-file generic applicants who have been awarded a 180-day exclusivity period do not unreasonably and indefinitely block subsequent generics from entering the market beyond the exclusivity period. The proposal makes the tentative approval of a subsequent generic drug applicant that is blocked solely by a first applicant's 180 day exclusivity, where the first applicant has not yet received final approval, a trigger of the first applicant's 180 day exclusivity. This means the period of exclusivity would immediately begin for the first filer. This proposal will enhance competition and facilitate more timely access to generic drugs.

Citations

[1] The Board of Trustees Federal Hospital Insurance and Federal Supplementary Medical Insurance Trust Funds: *2017 Annual Report of the Boards of Trustees of the Federal Hospital Insurance and Federal Supplementary Medicare Insurance Trust Funds*, (July 2017).

[2] Medicare Payment Advisory Commission: *Medicare and the Health Care Delivery System: Improving Medicare Part D*, Report to the Congress, (June 2016).

[3] The Henry J. Kaiser Family Foundation: *No Limit: Medicare Part D Enrollees Exposed to High Out-of-Pocket Drug Costs Without a Hard Cap on Spending*, (November 2017).

[4] Medicare Payment Advisory Commission: *Medicare and the Health Care Delivery System: Medicare Part B drug payment policy issues*, Report to the Congress, (June 2017).

MEDICARE: ELIMINATE WASTEFUL FEDERAL SPENDING
Department of Health and Human Services

The Budget includes a number of proposals that eliminate excessive spending and distortionary payment incentives without harming beneficiaries' access to care or altering covered items and services. It refines reimbursement for uncompensated and post-acute care, reforms competitive bidding for durable medical equipment, and eliminates higher out-of-pocket costs and unnecessarily high payments for services delivered at off-campus, hospital-owned physician offices. In addition, the Budget would establish prior authorization for certain physician self-referrals, limits hospital payments associated with early discharge to hospices, and increases savings from Accountable Care Organizations (ACO).

Funding Summary
(In millions of dollars)

	2019	2020	2021	2022	2023	2024	2025	2026	2027	2028	2019-23	2019-28
Consolidate GME payments	-370	-1,200	-2,090	-3,070	-4,120	-5,230	-6,270	-7,360	-8,580	-9,800	-10,850	-48,090
Reduce Medicare coverage of bad debts	-400	-1,330	-2,820	-3,760	-4,090	-4,350	-4,620	-4,910	-5,220	-5,530	-12,400	-37,030
Modify payments to hospitals for uncompensated care	0	-4,100	-5,180	-6,000	-6,870	-7,690	-8,540	-9,420	-10,370	-11,370	-22,150	-69,540
Address excessive payment for post-acute care providers by establishing a unified payment system based on patients' clinical needs rather than the site of care	-780	-1,960	-3,420	-5,820	-8,640	-9,650	-10,830	-11,800	-12,850	-14,440	-20,620	-80,190
Pay all hospital-owned physician offices located off-campus at the physician office rate	-1,240	-2,260	-2,510	-2,810	-3,140	-3,490	-3,860	-4,280	-4,750	-5,640	-11,960	-33,980
Address excessive hospital payments by reducing payment when patient quickly discharged to hospice	-70	-100	-110	-110	-120	-130	-140	-150	-160	-170	-510	-1,260
Expand basis for beneficiary assignment for ACOs	0	0	-10	-10	-20	-20	-20	-20	-20	-20	-40	-140
Allow ACOs to cover cost of primary care visits to encourage use of ACO's providers	0	-10	-10	-10	-10	-10	0	0	0	-10	-40	-60
Expand ability of MA organizations to pay for services delivered via telehealth	0	0	0	0	0	0	0	0	0	0	0	0
Reform/expand durable medical equipment competitive bidding	0	-330	-600	-630	-690	-740	-780	-840	-910	-960	-2,250	-6,480
Allow for Federal/State coordinated review of dual eligible Special Needs Plan marketing materials	0	0	0	0	0	0	0	0	0	0	0	0
Improve appeals notifications for dually eligible individuals in Integrated Health Plans	0	0	0	0	0	0	0	0	0	0	0	0
Clarify Part D SEP for dually eligible beneficiaries	-38	-53	-57	-62	-67	-72	-77	-83	-89	-95	-277	-693
Cancel funding from MIF	0	0	0	-193	0	0	0	0	0	0	-193	-193
Give beneficiaries with high deductible plans the option of tax deductible contributions to HSAs/MSAs	0	0	610	1,081	1,305	1,513	1,619	1,704	1,786	1,847	2,996	11,465
Total	-2,898	-11,343	-16,197	-21,394	-26,462	-29,869	-33,518	-37,159	-41,163	-46,188	-78,294	-266,191

Justification

The Budget includes two proposals aimed at reforming how the Government reimburses hospitals for certain "add-on" payments that are not directly tied to Medicare beneficiary care. These reforms improve the sustainability of the Medicare Trust Fund and ensure that Medicare funds are spent on meeting the health needs of our Nation's seniors. Additionally, these proposals better align the Medicare program with private sector health insurance business practices.

First, Medicare currently makes payments to hospitals related to uncompensated care for non-Medicare beneficiaries. The Budget proposes to reform uncompensated care payments by removing the payment from the Medicare payment system, moderating the rate of growth of spending, and establishing a new process to distribute uncompensated care amounts to hospitals based on their share of charity care and non-Medicare bad debt.

Second, the Federal Government spends more than \$15 billion annually in the Medicare, Medicaid, and Children's Graduate Medical Education (GME) programs with little to no accountability for outcomes. Experts have repeatedly recommended improving the distribution of funds to achieve a better distribution of specialties in health care, to address health care professional shortage areas, and to incentivize better training of professionals.[1,2] The Budget proposes to better focus Federal spending on training for health professionals by consolidating GME spending that is currently in the Medicare, Medicaid, and Children's Hospital GME Payment program into a new capped Federal grant program. Funding would be distributed to hospitals that are committed to building a strong medical workforce and would be targeted to address medically underserved communities and health professional shortages.

The Budget includes several additional proposals aimed at eliminating wasteful spending in Medicare.

Reduce Medicare coverage of bad debts—The Budget would reduce the amount Medicare pays to certain institutional providers to cover copayments or deductibles that beneficiaries fail to pay. Medicare currently reimburses certain providers at 65 percent of bad debt. Private insurance companies do not typically cover any portion of uncollected cost-sharing, which is the responsibility of the beneficiary. The Budget would bring Medicare more in line with the private sector by gradually reducing reimbursement to 25 percent of bad debt over three years.

Establish a unified payment system for post-acute care providers—Currently, Medicare uses separate prospective payment systems to pay for stays in the four main post-acute care settings: skilled nursing facilities; home health agencies; inpatient rehabilitation facilities; and long-term care hospitals. Non-partisan experts have repeatedly found that payment rates significantly exceed the costs of care in these settings, that payments do not align well with patients' clinical needs, and that patients may go to sites of care that provide more intensive services than are clinically necessary.[3]

Therefore, the Budget would transition payment for post-acute care to site-neutral payments over five years. It would reduce the growth rate of post-acute care payment during the transition period. The proposed payment system is based on the anticipated clinical needs and risk factors of the patient, rather than the site of service. All types of facilities would remain available, and patients with their doctors, would determine the right site of care.

Pay all hospital-owned physician offices located off-campus at the physician office rate—Most hospital-owned physician practices located off the hospital's main campus receive a higher payment rate from Medicare than practices not owned by hospitals. The Bipartisan Budget Act of 2015 addressed this inequity for new off-campus facilities, but grandfathered facilities in existence at the time. The Budget would equalize Medicare reimbursement for all physician practices and off-campus facilities, regardless of whether they are hospital-owned, lowering out-of-pocket costs for seniors receiving services at those facilities.

Address excessive hospital payments by reducing payment when a patient is quickly discharged to hospice—The Budget proposes to establish a hospital transfer policy when Medicare beneficiaries have shorter than average hospital stays prior to being transferred to hospice. In 2013, the HHS Office of Inspector General found that 30 percent of inpatient discharges to hospice would be classified as early discharges and that on average the Medicare payment was higher than the cost of care during that short stay.[6] This proposal would set Medicare payments at a rate more reflective of the resource intensity of the given stay and would better align with how Medicare pays early discharge to other facilities.

Increase savings from Accountable Care Organizations—ACOs are designed to help reduce wasteful Medicare spending and improve quality by coordinating patient care and preventing unnecessary duplication of services. The Budget proposes to provide additional flexibilities to increase savings through ACOs by enhancing beneficiary assignment and incentives. It would expand the basis for beneficiary assignment to a broader set of primary care providers, including nurse practitioners, physician assistants, and clinical nurse specialists, moving more beneficiaries from fee-for-service Medicare to value-based care, without affecting beneficiary access to providers or the care they receive. In addition, by allowing ACOs under two-sided risk to cover beneficiary cost-sharing for primary care visits, the Budget would encourage beneficiaries to engage in their care and make contact with ACO-affiliated providers.

Expand the ability of Medicare Advantage (MA) organizations to pay for services delivered via telehealth—Beginning in 2019, this proposal expands the ability of MA organizations to deliver medical services via telehealth by eliminating the requirement for MA organizations to provide specified covered Part B services exclusively through face-to-face encounters.

Require prior authorization when physicians order certain services excessively relative to their peers—Certain services that physicians offer to patients in their office (known as in-office ancillary services) are exempt from the physician self-referral law. Researchers, including the nonpartisan Medicare Payment Advisory Commission (MedPAC) and the Government Accountability Office, have found that physician self-referral of these in-office services are associated with higher volume than when these services are not self-referred.[4,][5] The Budget proposes to establish a targeted prior authorization program for certain in-office ancillary services that are prone to inappropriate physician self-referral and overutilization.

Reform and expand durable medical equipment competitive bidding—The Budget proposes to implement a more rational approach for setting payment rates in competitively bid areas by eliminating the single payment amount, and reimbursing winning durable medical suppliers at their bid amounts instead. This approach would incentivize suppliers to bid at an appropriate rate to acquire products and support their businesses. In addition, the Budget proposes to expand competitive bidding to all areas of the Nation. If an adequate number of suppliers do not participate in a bid area, rates from other similar areas would be used to set the payment amount in that bid area.

Reform physician self-referral law to better support and align with alternative payment models and to address overutilization—Physicians who participate in Advanced Alternative Payment Models may face some challenges related to physician self-referral law (the Stark Law). Effective CY 2020, this proposal would establish a new exception to the physician self-referral law for arrangements that arise due to participation in Advanced Alternative Payment Models. Additionally, this proposal would establish a new process for physicians to self-report inadvertent technical non-compliance violations of the law and this proposal excludes physician-owned distributors from the indirect compensation exception if more than 40 percent of the physician-owned distributor's business is generated by physician-owners.

Allow for Federal/State coordinated review of dual eligible Special Needs Plan marketing materials—Under current law, marketing materials provided by Dual Eligible Special Needs Plans to beneficiaries have to go through separate State and Center for Medicare and Medicaid Services (CMS) review processes. This proposal allows for joint state and CMS review, building on CMS's experience with joint review conducted under current demonstration authority. The proposal lowers administrative burden on participating plans and enhances their ability to provide a uniform message to beneficiaries.

Improve appeals notifications for dually eligible individuals in Integrated Health Plans—The Budget would provide HHS authority to streamline the appeals communication requirements for health plans that integrate payment and services for Medicare and Medicaid dually eligible enrollees, eliminating conflicting instructions that beneficiaries receive based on Medicare and Medicaid's differing requirements.

Clarify the Part D Special Enrollment Period for Dually Eligible Beneficiaries—Currently, enrollees who are entitled to Medicare Part A and Part B and are dually eligible for both Medicare and Medicaid have a continuous monthly special enrollment period (SEP) to request enrollment or disenrollment from a Medicare Part D prescription drug plan or MA plan outside of the annual enrollment period. Continuous ability to enroll and disenroll from a plan lessens the incentive for plans to invest in important care management or network development for these high cost and often vulnerable beneficiaries and creates significant inefficiencies for plans. The Budget would allow CMS to apply the same annual election process for both dually eligible and non-dually eligible beneficiaries but preserve the ability for dually eligible beneficiaries to use a SEP to opt into integrated care programs or to change plans following auto-assignment. Efficient use of the Part D SEP for full-benefit dual eligible beneficiaries would reduce aggressive marketing targeted to low-income beneficiaries, improve incentives to make investments in and provide care coordination for high-cost, often vulnerable beneficiaries, and reduce the administrative burden on health plans when beneficiaries fluctuate numerous times throughout the year.

Cancel funding from the Medicare Improvement Fund (MIF)—Since the creation of the MIF in 2008, the Congress has added to or rescinded funding from the MIF as needed to provide offsets for statutory changes. The Budget proposes to rescind the amounts currently available in the MIF and use these amounts to create savings for Medicare.

Give Medicare beneficiaries with high deductible health plans the option to make tax deductible contributions to Health Savings Accounts and Medical Savings Accounts—Currently Medicare beneficiaries in high-deductible health plans are not allowed to make tax-deductible contributions to their Health Savings Accounts (HSAs) or Medicare Savings Accounts (MSAs). This proposal would give Medicare beneficiaries greater flexibility to take control of their health. It would allow beneficiaries enrolled in Medicare MSA Plans to contribute to their MSAs, subject to the annual HSA contribution limits as determined by the Internal Revenue Service. Beneficiaries would also have a one-time opportunity to roll over the funds from their private HSAs to their Medicare MSAs. Beneficiaries who elect this plan option would not be allowed to purchase Medigap or other supplemental insurance. Medicare beneficiaries who have an employer-sponsored high-deductible health would also be allowed to make contributions to their HSAs, although Medicare would not cover any of the deductible.

Citations

[1] Medicare Payment Advisory Commission: *Aligning Incentives in Medicare: Graduate Medical Education Financing: Focusing on Educational Priorities*, Report to the Congress, (June 2010).

[2] National Academies of Sciences: *Engineering, and Medicine, Graduate Medical Education That Meets the Nation's Health Needs*, (July 2014).

[3] Medicare Payment Advisory Commission: *Medicare Payment Policy: Chapters 8-11,* Report to the Congress, (June 2016).

[4] Medicare Payment Advisory Commission: *Medicare and the Health Care Delivery System: Improving payment accuracy and appropriate use of ancillary services*, Report to the Congress, (June 2011).

[5] Government Accountability Office: *Self-Referring Providers Generally Referred More Beneficiaries but Fewer Services per Beneficiary*, GAO-14-270, (April, 2014).

[6] Health and Human Services Office of Inspector General: *Medicare Could Save Millions by Implementing a Hospital Transfer Payment Policy for Early Discharges to Hospice Care*, A-01-12-005-7, (May 2013).

REDUCE THE GRACE PERIOD FOR EXCHANGE PREMIUMS
Department of Health and Human Services

Under current law, individuals receiving advance payment of the premium tax credit (APTC) for their enrollment in Exchange plans have a 90-day grace period. This proposal would reduce the 90-day grace period for individuals on Exchange plans to repay any missed premium payments to 30 days.

Funding Summary
(In millions of dollars)

	2019	2020	2021	2022	2023	2024	2025	2026	2027	2028	2019-23	2019-28
Proposed Change from Current Law..........................	-975	-325	0	0	0	0	0	0	0	0	-1,300	-1,300

Justification

Under current law, individuals receiving advance payment of the premium tax credit (APTC) for their enrollment in Exchange plans have a 90-day grace period. Before Obamacare, grace periods were determined and varied by State laws. Obamacare established a 90-day grace period, allowing consumers to repay any missed premium payments before they are terminated from plan enrollment during this 90-day period. This proposal reduces the grace period to 30 days, resulting in a reduction in the Federal deficit.

STRENGTHEN THE CHILD SUPPORT ENFORCEMENT PROGRAM
Department of Health and Human Services

The Budget includes a number of proposals that strengthen the Child Support Enforcement Program, which would provide State agencies additional tools to increase efficiency, facilitate family self-sufficiency, and promote responsible parenthood.

Funding Summary
(In millions of dollars)

	2019	2020	2021	2022	2023	2024	2025	2026	2027	2028	2019-23	2019-28
Strengthen Child Support enforcement and establishment.........................	-22	-42	-57	-68	-76	-80	-82	-82	-83	-94	-265	-686
Establish a Child Support Technology Fund...................	63	-12	-20	-28	-37	-110	-120	-131	-194	-205	-34	-794
Get non-custodial parents to work...	4	5	7	8	10	9	11	13	14	15	34	96
Total...	45	-49	-70	-88	-103	-181	-191	-200	-263	-284	-265	-1,384

Justification

The package of child support enforcement and establishment proposals in the Budget would increase child support collections that would in turn result in savings to Federal benefits programs. For example, by requiring additional data matches and reporting throughout child support establishment and enforcement processes, the proposal expands the ability to intercept sources of income for payment of child support, including insurance settlements, lump-sum payments provided by employers, gaming winnings from casinos, and State workers' compensation claims. The package also improves enforcement procedures related to freezing and seizing certain assets held by delinquent non-custodial parents, and would require the reporting of independent contractors to State directories used to locate non-custodial parents and identify sources of income. Finally, the package of proposals provides States and Tribes with access to better financial data matching programs, as well as tools that promote interstate cooperation.

In addition, the Budget includes a proposal to create a Child Support Technology Fund to facilitate the needed replacement of aging IT systems in State child support programs, and increase security, efficiency, and program integrity. Incorporating the advantages of private sector approaches to operating Government programs, the proposal leverages reusable technology to create savings and cost-efficiencies for the States and Federal Government and to provide better service delivery to child support customers. Specifically, the proposed approach reduces inefficiencies associated with the current process of modernizing child support IT systems, which involves each State separately designing, developing, and implementing a new system, with costs averaging $120 million per State. The Federal Government shares these costs through 66 percent Federal reimbursement. Under the Budget proposal, States would use a new generation statewide system that will be purchased by HHS, allowing the Federal Government to avoid reimbursing up to 54 times over the costs associated with building new State systems.

Finally, the Budget proposes to get non-custodial parents to work by expanding the work requirement in the Child Support Enforcement Program, while allowing for limited Federal funding to support employment and training services for non-custodial parents who are behind in their child support payments. The proposal recognizes that mandated work requirement for this population is an evidence-based and cost-effective approach to obtaining regular child support payments. It promotes personal responsibility, enables non-custodial parents to provide for their children, and allows their families to avoid Government dependence.

TEMPORARY ASSISTANCE FOR NEEDY FAMILIES REFORMS
Department of Health and Human Services

The Budget proposes to promote State innovation in strengthening the safety net through Welfare to Work Projects. The Budget would also reduce the Temporary Assistance for Needy Families (TANF) block grant by 10 percent, which is the portion that States may transfer from TANF to Social Services Block Grant (SSBG), and proposes to eliminate the TANF Contingency Fund, as it fails to provide well-targeted counter-cyclical funding to States. Accompanying these proposed cuts is a package of legislative proposals to improve the TANF program by strengthening its primary performance measure related to work engagement, and ensuring that States allocate sufficient funds to work, education, and training activities.

Funding Summary
(In millions of dollars)

	2019	2020	2021	2022	2023	2024	2025	2026	2027	2028	2019-23	2019-28
Reduce TANF block grant.......	-1,155	-1,435	-1,514	-1,552	-1,584	-1,600	-1,600	-1,600	-1,600	-1,600	-7,240	-15,240
Eliminate the TANF Contingency Fund.................	-545	-608	-608	-608	-608	-608	-608	-608	-608	-608	-2,977	-6,017
Strengthen TANF.................	0	0	0	0	0	0	0	0	0		0	0
Promote Welfare to Work Projects............................	0	0	0	0	0	0	0	0	0	0	0	0
Total..	-1,700	-2,043	-2,122	-2,160	-2,192	-2,208	-2,208	-2,208	-2,208	-2,208	-10,217	-21,257

Justification

Recognizing the value of state innovation in strengthening America's safety net, the Budget provides states with the opportunity to propose Welfare to Work Projects that streamline funding from multiple public assistance programs, and provide services that are tailored to their constituents' specific needs. By holding States accountable for achieving targeted outcomes that focus on fostering employment, reducing welfare dependency, and promoting child and family well-being, these projects will serve to build the evidence base of best practices for helping low-income individuals achieve self-sufficiency.

The Budget would also reduce the Temporary Assistance for Needy Families (TANF) block grant by 10 percent, which is the portion that States may transfer from TANF to Social Services Block Grant (SSBG). While this proposal reduces the amount available to States for cash assistance and other benefits that promote self-sufficiency, it also recognizes that TANF's flexible spending rules have resulted in States using a large portion of TANF funds for benefits and services that do not directly serve the core intent of the program to help low-income families meet their basic needs and move them towards self-sufficiency. To reverse this pattern, the Budget would ensure sufficient TANF investments in work promotion activities by adding a requirement that States spend at least 30 percent of federal TANF and state maintenance-of-effort funds on: work, education, and training activities; work supports, including child care; and assessment/service provision for TANF eligible families. The Budget also proposes key changes to TANF's primary performance measure related to work engagement, which will further strengthen the program's accountability and effectiveness. These changes include (1) replacing the Caseload Reduction Credit with an Employment Credit that rewards states for moving TANF recipients to work; (2) collapsing the two work participation rates into one standard rate that measures work engagement for families; and (3) allowing states to count partial credit to incentivize states to increase work participation among all families.

Finally, the Budget proposes to eliminate the TANF Contingency Fund, recognizing its failure to provide well-targeted counter-cyclical funding to States. While the intent of the Contingency Fund has been to assist States experiencing increased demand for cash assistance during economic downturns, States may use contingency funds for any TANF purpose, many of which have no direct relationship to helping families meet needs in hard economic times. Some States have used contingency funds to simply replace existing block grant funds (i.e., building up their unobligated balances), without actually spending more to address increased need. In addition, because the triggers for eligibility for the Contingency Fund have not been updated, all States except Wyoming have been eligible for the Fund in every month since June 2009.

ESTABLISH AN IMMIGRATION SERVICES SURCHARGE
Department of Homeland Security

The Budget proposes to add a 10 percent surcharge on all requests received by U.S. Citizenship and Immigration Services (USCIS), including applications for citizenship, adjustment of status, and petitions for temporary workers. These collections would be deposited into the General Fund of the U.S. Treasury for deficit reduction.

Funding Summary
(In millions of dollars)

	2019	2020	2021	2022	2023	2024	2025	2026	2027	2028	2019-23	2019-28
Proposed Change from Current Law..........................	-453	-465	-479	-493	-507	-522	-538	-553	-569	-587	-2,397	-5,166

Justification

Those who request immigration services derive benefits beyond the direct costs to the Federal Government of adjudicating those requests. Consistent with this, the Budget would ensure that these requestors contribute to deficit reduction.

EXTEND EXPIRING CUSTOMS AND BORDER PROTECTION FEES
Department of Homeland Security

This proposal would re-authorize Customs User Fees set to expire on September 30, 2025.

Funding Summary
(In millions of dollars)

	2019	2020	2021	2022	2023	2024	2025	2026	2027	2028	2019-23	2019-28
Proposed Change from Current Law..........................	0	0	0	0	0	0	0	-3,406	-4,556	-4,796	0	-12,758

Justification

The Budget proposes to extend the Merchandise Processing Fee beyond its current expiration date of January 14, 2026 to January 14, 2031. It also proposes to extend statutorily set Consolidated Omnibus Budget Reconciliation Act of 1985 (COBRA) fees, and the Express Consignment Courier Facilities (ECCF) fee created under the Trade Act of 2002, beyond their current expiration date of September 30, 2025 to September 30, 2030.

INCREASE CUSTOMS USER FEES
Department of Homeland Security

The Budget proposes to increase Consolidated Omnibus Budget Reconciliation Act of 1985 (COBRA), and Express Consignment Courier Facilities (ECCF) fees, and adjust for inflation.

Funding Summary
(In millions of dollars)

	2019	2020	2021	2022	2023	2024	2025	2026	2027	2028	2019-23	2019-28
Proposed Change from Current Law...............	-113	-126	-137	-148	-162	-176	-191	-206	-223	-214	-686	-1,696

Justification

The Budget proposes to increase statutorily set COBRA fees and the ECCF fee created under the Trade Act of 2002. COBRA created a series of user fees for air and sea passengers; commercial trucks; railroad cars; private aircraft and vessels; commercial vessels; dutiable mail packages; broker permits; barges and bulk carriers from Canada and Mexico; cruise vessel passengers; and ferry vessel passengers. This proposal would increase the customs inspection fee by $2.10 for certain air and sea passengers and increase other COBRA fees by proportional amounts. The additional revenue raised from increasing the user fees will allow the U.S. Customs and Border Protection (CBP) to recover more costs associated with customs-related inspections, and reduce waiting times by helping to support the hiring of 840 new CBP Officers. This fee was last adjusted in April 2007, yet international travel volumes have grown since that time and CBP costs for customs inspections continue to increase. As a result, CBP relies on its annually appropriated funds to support the difference between fee collections and the costs of providing customs inspectional services. The Government Accountability Office's most recent review of these COBRA user fees (July 2016) identified that CBP collected $686 million in COBRA/ECCF fees compared to $870 million in operating costs, exhibiting a recovery rate of 78 percent.[1] With the fee increase, CBP would potentially collect the same amount it incurs in COBRA/ECCF eligible costs in 2019. The proposed legislation will close the gap between costs and collections, enabling CBP to provide improved inspectional services to those who pay this user fee.

Citations

[1] General Accountability Office, *Enhanced Oversight Could Better Ensure Programs Receiving Fees and Other Collections Use Funds Efficiently,* GAO-16-443, (July 2016)

INCREASE WORKSITE ENFORCEMENT PENALTIES
Department of Homeland Security

The Administration proposes to increase by 35 percent all penalty amounts charged against employers who violate Immigration and Nationality Act provisions on the unlawful employment of aliens.

Funding Summary
(In millions of dollars)

	2019	2020	2021	2022	2023	2024	2025	2026	2027	2028	2019-23	2019-28
Proposed Change from Current Law........................	-13	-14	-15	-15	-15	-15	-15	-15	-15	-15	-72	-147

Justification

According to 2012 estimates, there are some 8.1 million unauthorized workers in the U.S. civilian labor force. As U.S. Immigration and Customs Enforcement increases its efforts to stop businesses from employing those who should not be working in the U.S., the Administration proposes increasing by 35 percent the fines and penalties charged to those employers found to be violating the law.

REAUTHORIZE OIL SPILL LIABILITY TRUST FUND EXCISE TAX
Department of Homeland Security

The Budget proposes to reauthorize the per barrel oil tax that expired on December 31, 2017.

Funding Summary
(In millions of dollars)

	2019	2020	2021	2022	2023	2024	2025	2026	2027	2028	2019-23	2019-28
Proposed Change from Current Law..........................	-354	-466	-473	-480	-489	-494	-500	-507	-511	-511	-2,262	-4,785

Justification

On December 31, 2017, the per barrel excise tax on oil expired. This tax is deposited into the Oil Spill Liability Trust Fund, which provides funding for Federal cleanup and response efforts for oil spills in U.S. waters. The Budget proposes to reinstate this tax at the same rate as when it expired, in order to continue to guarantee adequate resources on hand in the case of a truly catastrophic oil spill on the same scale as Deepwater Horizon.

CANCEL SOUTHERN NEVADA PUBLIC LANDS MANAGEMENT ACT BALANCES
Department of the Interior

The Budget proposes to cancel $230 million in unobligated balances in a special account established under the Southern Nevada Public Lands Management Act (SNPLMA), which has already generated over $3 billion to address the most important projects in Nevada.

Funding Summary
(In millions of dollars)

	2019	2020	2021	2022	2023	2024	2025	2026	2027	2028	2019-23	2019-28
Proposed Change from Current Law...........................	-83	-69	-78	0	0	0	0	0	0	0	-230	-230

Justification

Enacted in 1998, SNPLMA authorizes the Bureau of Land Management (BLM) to sell specified public lands around Las Vegas, NV, and retain 85 percent of the proceeds in a special account to use for capital improvements and various conservation, restoration, and recreational purposes at the discretion of the Secretary of the Interior. Since its enactment, the Department of the Interior has received over $3.4 billion from land sales under SNPLMA authority, and the proceeds have funded over 1,200 conservation, restoration, and infrastructure projects across Southern Nevada, with notable investments in Lakes Tahoe and Mead. However, in recent years the program is increasingly in search of qualified 'critical need' projects, which has led to lingering unobligated balances. This proposal would only reduce a portion of the over $600 million in remaining balances and would not affect any specific projects currently identified.

REAUTHORIZE THE FEDERAL LAND TRANSACTION FACILITATION ACT
Department of the Interior

This proposal would permanently reauthorize the Federal Land Transaction Facilitation Act (FLTFA), which expired in 2011. FLTFA facilitates the disposal of surplus lands, as identified in the Department of the Interior's Bureau of Land Management (BLM) and the Department of Agriculture's Forest Service (USFS) management plans, by allowing BLM and USFS to use the receipts to acquire 'high conservation value' lands.

Funding Summary
(In millions of dollars)

	2019	2020	2021	2022	2023	2024	2025	2026	2027	2028	2019-23	2019-28
Proposed Change from Current Law..........................	-5	-6	-9	-12	-3	0	0	0	0	0	-35	-35

Justification

The proposal would reauthorize FLTFA to allow BLM and USFS to retain receipts from the sale of lands identified as suitable for disposal in recent land use plans and then use the funds to acquire environmentally sensitive lands. First enacted in 2000, FLTFA encouraged BLM and USFS to sell or exchange public lands identified for disposal, while at the same time, provided an alternative source of funds to acquire sensitive lands, such as inholdings or parcels that provide access to public lands for hunters and anglers. Before the authorization expired in 2011, FLTFA required that 80 percent of the receipts be spent in the same State in which the funds were generated, with the remaining funds available for acquisition in any of the 11 other Western States. The current proposal would continue this requirement.

REPEAL ENHANCED GEOTHERMAL PAYMENTS TO COUNTIES
Department of the Interior

The Budget proposes to repeal Section 224(b) of the Energy Policy Act of 2005 to permanently discontinue payments to counties and restore the disposition of Federal geothermal leasing revenues to the historical formula of 50 percent to the States and 50 percent to the U.S. Treasury.

Funding Summary
(In millions of dollars)

	2019	2020	2021	2022	2023	2024	2025	2026	2027	2028	2019-23	2019-28
Proposed Change from Current Law...........................	-4	-4	-4	-4	-4	-4	-4	-4	-4	-4	-20	-40

Justification

The Energy Policy Act of 2005 changed the distribution of receipts from geothermal leases to provide 50 percent to States, 25 percent to counties, and 25 to the Federal Government. In almost all other situations where leasing revenues are generated on Federal lands, the receipts are split between the Federal Government and the affected State. The extra 25 percent in county payments are inconsistent with this longstanding revenue-sharing approach, and effectively reduce the return to Federal taxpayers from geothermal leases on Federal lands.

ESTABLISH AN UNEMPLOYMENT INSURANCE SOLVENCY STANDARD
Department of Labor

States are responsible for funding the benefits they provide under the State-administered Unemployment Insurance (UI) program. In order to avoid raising taxes on employers in the middle of a recession, States should build balances that would allow them to cover benefits when unemployment spikes. However, despite years of recovery since the Great Recession, many States' UI accounts are still not adequately financed—as of September 30, 2017, only 24 States had sufficient reserves to weather another recession. The Budget proposes to strengthen the incentive for States to prepare for the next recession and adequately fund their UI systems by reducing Federal tax credits in States with particularly low reserve balances.

Funding Summary
(In millions of dollars)

	2019	2020	2021	2022	2023	2024	2025	2026	2027	2028	2019-23	2019-28
Proposed Change from Current Law...............	0	0	-633	-1,615	-2,230	-919	-1,613	-927	-1,267	-1,907	-4,478	-11,111

Justification

States are expected to build up sufficient reserves in their UI programs during non-recessionary periods to allow them to pay for benefits during the next recession. When States fail to build up sufficient balances, they either need to increase taxes on employers in the middle of a recession or borrow from the Federal Government, which can trigger increased taxes on employers through automatic Federal Unemployment Tax Act "credit reductions."

Currently, fewer than half the States have sufficient reserves to cover a full year of benefits during a recession—the common measure of State solvency in the UI program. The Budget proposes to encourage States to build up reserves in their Unemployment Trust Fund accounts by implementing a minimum solvency standard, equal to the level of reserves that would be sufficient to pay six months of benefits during an average recession (half of the common solvency target). This proposal would impose credit reductions on States that fail to meet the solvency standard for two consecutive years rather than only imposing the credit reduction once States have been borrowing from the Federal Government for two consecutive years. This would strengthen States' incentive to adequately fund their UI systems before their Trust Funds face any future recessionary demands, resulting in a decrease in the likelihood of insolvency and the need to borrow. All funds received through the credit reduction would be applied to State Unemployment Trust Fund accounts to help States rebuild balances.

IMPROVE PENSION BENEFIT GUARANTY CORPORATION SOLVENCY
Department of Labor

The Budget proposes to improve the solvency of the Pension Benefit Guaranty Corporation (PBGC) by increasing the insurance premiums paid by underfunded multiemployer pension plans. PBGC premiums are currently far lower than what a private financial institution would charge for insuring the same risk. The proposed premium reforms would improve PBGC's financial condition and are expected to be sufficient to fund the multiemployer program for the next 20 years.

Funding Summary
(In millions of dollars)

	2019	2020	2021	2022	2023	2024	2025	2026	2027	2028	2019-23	2019-28
Proposed Change from Current Law..........................	74	-1,470	-1,564	-1,663	-1,760	-1,810	1,428	-5,128	-1,901	-1,936	-6,383	-15,730

Justification

PBGC provides pension insurance for private sector defined benefit retirement plans through single-employer and multiemployer programs. PBGC collects premiums that are set by the Congress separately for each of the programs. Under the multiemployer insurance program, when a plan runs out of money, PBGC provides financial assistance to the plan so that the plan can pay benefits at no more than the guarantee level.

While the single-employer program is on the path towards solvency, the multiemployer program, covering over 10 million participants, is in dire financial condition. The 2017 multiemployer program deficit was $65.1 billion, with only $2 billion in assets and $67 billion in liabilities. PBGC projects the multiemployer program will be insolvent by the end of 2025, at which point participants in insolvent plans would see their benefits cut by as much as 90 percent. Multiemployer premiums are very low-a flat rate of just $28 per participant in 2018. In order to better align multiemployer premiums with the risk PBGC is insuring and prevent insolvency, the Budget proposes to create a variable-rate premium (VRP)—as exists in the single-employer program—and an exit premium.

The multiemployer VRP would require plans to pay an additional premium based on their level of underfunding, up to a cap that would be indexed to inflation. PBGC would have limited authority to design waivers for terminated plans, or plans that are in critical status, if there is a substantial risk that the payment of premiums would accelerate plan insolvency and result in earlier financial assistance.

An exit premium, equal to 10 times the VRP cap, would be assessed on employers that withdraw from a plan to compensate the insurance program for the additional risk imposed on it when employers leave the system and cease making plan contributions. Employers who withdraw from a multiemployer plan pay a withdrawal liability to the plan, but this payment is typically insufficient to cover the employer's share of the plan's unfunded liabilities.

REFORM THE FEDERAL EMPLOYEES' COMPENSATION ACT (FECA)
Department of Labor

The Federal Employees' Compensation Act (FECA) program provides wage replacement and medical benefits to Federal civilian employees who suffer from occupational injury or disease, or to their survivors. The Budget proposes to reform the program and generate cost savings by simplifying FECA benefit rates, modernizing benefit administration, and enhancing controls to prevent fraud and limit improper payments.

Funding Summary
(In millions of dollars)

	2019	2020	2021	2022	2023	2024	2025	2026	2027	2028	2019-23	2019-28
Proposed Change from Current Law............	-62	-7	-5	-5	-5	-6	-6	-8	-8	-5	-84	-117

Justification

FECA has not been substantially updated since 1974. The FECA program pays two-thirds of the individual's basic pay, but up to 75 percent for individuals with dependents, higher than the majority of State workers' compensation programs. This compensation is adjusted for inflation annually and not taxed. FECA benefits typically exceed Federal retirement benefits, enticing individuals to remain on FECA past when they would otherwise have retired. Individuals can receive FECA benefits indefinitely, as long as their injury or illness diminishes their wage-earning capacity.

The Budget proposal would reform the FECA program prospectively to provide a single rate of compensation for new injuries at 66 2/3 percent of the injured workers' pay; convert retirement-age beneficiaries to a retirement annuity-level benefit; establish an up-front waiting period for benefits for all beneficiaries; increase benefits for disfigurement and burial; suspend payments to indicted medical providers; and make other changes to improve the program integrity and reduce improper payments. A number of these reforms echo longstanding Department of Labor Inspector General and Government Accountability Office recommendations.

REFORM THE TRADE ADJUSTMENT ASSISTANCE PROGRAM
Department of Labor

The Trade Adjustment Assistance (TAA) program, which provides cash benefits and training to workers who have been displaced by international trade, is in need of reform. A 2012 evaluation of the program demonstrated that program participants were slightly worse off than non-participants at the end of a four-year follow-up period. The Budget proposes legislative changes to refocus the TAA program on apprenticeship and on-the-job training, earn-as-you-learn strategies that ensure that participants are getting job-relevant training.

Funding Summary
(In millions of dollars)

	2019	2020	2021	2022	2023	2024	2025	2026	2027	2028	2019-23	2019-28
Proposed Change from Current Law..........................	-98	-211	-318	-281	-260	-158	-77	-81	-112	-148	-1,168	-1,744

Justification

A rigorous 2012 evaluation of the TAA program demonstrated that workers who participated in the program had lower earnings than the comparison group at the end of a four-year follow-up period, in part because they were more likely to participate in long-term job training programs rather than immediately reentering the workforce.[1] However, this training was not targeted to in-demand industries and occupations—only 37 percent of participants became employed in the occupations for which they trained. The Budget proposes to refocus the TAA program on apprenticeship and on-the-job training, earn-as-you-learn strategies that would improve participants' workforce outcomes by helping to place them in relevant occupations. States would also be encouraged to place a greater emphasis on intensive reemployment services for workers who are not participating in work-based training, getting those individuals back into the workforce more quickly.

Citations

[1] Mathematica Policy Research, Inc., and Social Policy Research Associates: *The Evaluation of the Trade Adjustment Assistance Program*, (December 2012).

DEBT COLLECTION PROPOSALS
Department of the Treasury

The Budget includes two legislative proposals that would authorize the Department of the Treasury (Treasury) to collect more debt that is due to the Federal Government.

Funding Summary
(In millions of dollars)

	2019	2020	2021	2022	2023	2024	2025	2026	2027	2028	2019-23	2019-28
Increase Delinquent Federal Non-tax Debt Collections	-32	-32	-32	-32	-32	-32	-32	-32	-32	-32	-160	-320
Increase and Streamline Recovery of Unclaimed Assets.................................	-8	-8	-8	-8	-8	-8	-8	-8	-8	-8	-40	-80

Justification

Increase delinquent Federal non-tax debt collections by authorizing administrative bank garnishment for non-tax debts of commercial entities—This proposal would allow Federal agencies to collect delinquent non-tax debt by garnishing the accounts of delinquent commercial debtors without a court order after providing full administrative due process. The proposal is modeled on existing authority for the Internal Revenue Service to collect Federal tax debts. In addition to providing appropriate limitations, the legislation would direct the Secretary of the Treasury to issue Government-wide regulations implementing the authority of bank garnishment for non-tax debts of commercial entities.

Increase and streamline recovery of unclaimed assets owed to the United States by authorizing Treasury to locate and recover these assets—This proposal would authorize Treasury to recover unclaimed assets and to retain a portion of amounts collected to pay for the costs of recovery. States and other entities hold assets in the name of the United States or in the name of departments, agencies, and other subdivisions of the Federal Government. Many agencies are not recovering these assets due to lack of expertise and funding. While unclaimed Federal assets are generally not considered to be delinquent debts, Treasury's debt collection operations personnel have the skills and training to recover these assets.

INCREASE AND EXTEND GUARANTEE FEE CHARGED BY GSES
Department of the Treasury

The Budget proposes to increase the guarantee fee charged by Fannie Mae and Freddie Mac from 0.10 to 0.20 percentage points from 2019 through 2021, and extend the 0.20 percentage point fee through 2023. This proposal is expected to generate approximately $26 billion over the 10-year Budget window.

Funding Summary
(In millions of dollars)

	2019	2020	2021	2022	2023	2024	2025	2026	2027	2028	2019-23	2019-28
Proposed Change from Current Law..........................	-212	-967	-1,699	-2,350	-3,475	-4,258	-4,034	-3,398	-2,858	-2,401	-8,703	-25,652

Justification

Under current law, Fannie Mae and Freddie Mac (Government Sponsored Enterprises or GSEs) impose a 0.10 percentage point fee above and beyond their normal guarantee fees that is collected and remitted to the U.S. Treasury for deficit reduction pursuant to the Temporary Payroll Tax Cut Continuation Act of 2011 (TPTCCA). This existing TPTCCA fee is currently in effect through 2021 and generates approximately $38 billion in deficit savings over the 10-year Budget window. This proposal would help to level the playing field for private lenders seeking to compete with the GSEs.

PROVIDE AUTHORITY FOR BUREAU OF ENGRAVING AND PRINTING TO CONSTRUCT A NEW FACILITY
Department of the Treasury

The Budget proposes to provide authority to the Bureau of Engraving and Printing (BEP) to construct a more efficient production facility.

Funding Summary
(In millions of dollars)

	2019	2020	2021	2022	2023	2024	2025	2026	2027	2028	2019-23	2019-28
Proposed Change from Current Law............................	-12	-32	-3	89	-360	-53	20	-3	-222	-3	-318	-579

Justification

BEP's current production facility in Washington, D.C. is an aging and outdated building that cannot accommodate the basic requirements of modern currency production and requires costly renovations. Purchasing and constructing a new facility would be less expensive and would make the manufacturing process more efficient. However, under current law, BEP does not have the authority to purchase or construct a new production facility. This proposal would allow BEP to purchase and construct a new facility, resulting in savings to the Federal Government.

REQUIRE SSN FOR CHILD TAX CREDIT & EARNED INCOME TAX CREDIT
Department of the Treasury

The Budget proposes requiring a Social Security Number (SSN) that is valid for work in order to claim the Earned Income Tax Credit (EITC) or the Child Tax Credit (CTC). For both credits, this requirement would apply to taxpayers, spouses, and all qualifying children. Under current law, households who do not have SSNs that are valid for work, including illegal immigrants who use Individual Taxpayer Identification Numbers, may claim the CTC, including the refundable portion, as long as the children for whom the credit is claimed have a SSN. This proposal would ensure that only individuals who are authorized to work in the United States could claim these credits by extending the SSN requirement for children to parents on the tax form. While this requirement is already current law for the EITC, this proposal would fix an administrative gap to strengthen enforcement of the provision.

Funding Summary
(In millions of dollars)

	2019	2020	2021	2022	2023	2024	2025	2026	2027	2028	2019-23	2019-28
Proposed Change from Current Law..........................	-1,186	-1,218	-1,164	-1,086	-1,104	-1,009	-921	-903	-790	-702	-5,758	-10,083

Justification

The Budget would ensure that only taxpayers who are authorized to work in the United States receive the EITC and CTC. This proposal would also fix gaps in the current administrative practice for EITC filers that allowed some people who have SSNs that are not valid for work to still claim the EITC. Since the EITC is a work support, only those people who are lawfully eligible to work in the United States should be able to claim it.

CAP POST-9/11 GI BILL FLIGHT TRAINING AT PUBLIC SCHOOLS
Department of Veterans Affairs

Under the Post-9/11 GI Bill, the Department of Veterans Affairs (VA) pays full tuition and fees for eligible veterans at public institutions of higher learning. Some flight training programs offered through these institutions (often at private, contracted schools) are much more expensive than other courses of study, often surpassing the maximum benefit level provided by the GI Bill. This proposal would cap the maximum benefit for all VA funded flight programs at the private school benefit cap (currently about $22,800 per year).

Funding Summary
(In millions of dollars)

	2019	2020	2021	2022	2023	2024	2025	2026	2027	2028	2019-23	2019-28
Proposed Change from Current Law...............	-43	-45	-46	-47	-49	-51	-53	-55	-57	-59	-230	-505

Justification

The Post-9/11 GI Bill provides eligible veterans with full tuition and fees at public universities, and tuition and fees at private universities up to a cap of about $22,800 per year. Over the past several years, certain public schools have been offering flight training, often through contracts with private institutions at a cost significantly higher than other courses of study. Capping the benefit at the maximum benefit provided for private schools would maintain a robust benefit but would reduce the likelihood that VA would pay excessive amounts for these programs. The savings from this proposal are designated to partially offset the costs of unifying the veterans community care program.

REINSTATE COLA ROUND DOWN
Department of Veterans Affairs

For nearly 15 years, until 2013, the Department of Veterans Affairs (VA) rounded down payment rates to all disability compensation beneficiaries. This proposal would reestablish the practice of rounding down to the nearest dollar the annual Cost Of Living Adjustments (COLA) for service-connected disability compensation, dependency and indemnity compensation, and certain education programs. This proposal would use the resulting savings to ensure a smooth transition to the unified veteran community care program, beginning in 2019.

Funding Summary
(In millions of dollars)

	2019	2020	2021	2022	2023	2024	2025	2026	2027	2028	2019-23	2019-28
Proposed Change from Current Law............................	-34	-92	-148	-207	-268	-281	-296	-311	-323	-336	-749	-2,296

Justification

Each year, veterans in receipt of certain disability benefits receive a yearly COLA increase to ensure that the purchasing power of VA benefits is not eroded by inflation. For nearly 15 years, until 2013, VA rounded down payment rates to all disability compensation beneficiaries. This proposal would reinstate that round-down, which has only a minimal impact, estimated at no more than $12 per year on individual veterans. The savings from this proposal are designated to partially offset the costs of unifying the veterans community care program.

STANDARDIZE & ENHANCE VA COMPENSATION & PENSION BENEFIT PROGRAMS
Department of Veterans Affairs

This set of proposals removes veterans annual income from their net worth calculation, helping standardize and automate benefits calculation, changing the required threshold for the Department of Veterans Affairs (VA) to perform some clinical medical evaluations, and expands VA's authority to re-issue benefits to veterans victimized by fiduciary misconduct.

Funding Summary
(In millions of dollars)

	2019	2020	2021	2022	2023	2024	2025	2026	2027	2028	2019-23	2019-28
Proposed Change from Current Law............	-78	-80	-83	-85	-88	-90	-93	-95	-98	-397	-414	-1,187

Justification

These proposals help rationalize and standardize VA disability compensation to benefit veterans. First, when calculating veterans' net worth, VA would no longer count annual income in the total. This helps VA standardize the calculation and potentially automate payments, allowing veterans to get payments faster. Second, VA would change the required threshold to perform some clinically unnecessary medical evaluations. Over the last several years, court precedents have required VA to order medical examinations with little to no medical or other objective evidence showing their necessity. In recent years, the courts have held that evidence necessary to satisfy the claim requirements is much lower than VA or the Congress contemplated. As a result, VA estimates nearly 180,000 medical exams were unnecessarily performed during 2016. This proposal aims to eliminate delays in claims processing by establishing a more reasonable policy in determining when a VA examination is warranted in connection with a claim for compensation. VA would also reissue benefits to veterans victimized by fiduciary misconduct.

STANDARDIZE & IMPROVE VETERAN VOCATIONAL REHABILITATION AND EDUCATION BENEFIT PROGRAMS
Department of Veterans Affairs

These proposals revise and standardize the Department of Veterans Affairs (VA) authorities for vocational rehabilitation and education programs to provide improved service and benefits to veterans.

Funding Summary
(In millions of dollars)

	2019	2020	2021	2022	2023	2024	2025	2026	2027	2028	2019-23	2019-28
Proposed Change from Current Law............................	72	-20	-22	-25	-26	-33	-35	-37	-39	-41	-21	-206

Justification

These proposals revise and standardize VA authorities for vocational rehabilitation and education programs. VA is proposing to lengthen the maximum time veterans may receive vocational rehabilitation services from 18 to 24 months; require States to offer vocational rehabilitation recipients the same tuition rates available to all other veterans; and extend VA's authority to provide vocational rehabilitation for service members with a serious illness or injury who have not yet received a VA service-connected disability compensation rating. In most cases, these individuals will eventually receive such a rating, and this authority improves their transition from the armed forces into civilian life. VA would also be able to approve preparatory courses for licensing and certification exams for GI Bill benefits. Currently, VA can reimburse costs of fees associated with licensing and certification exams required to enter into, maintain, or advance in a given vocation or profession (e.g., State bar exams, medical board exams, electrician exams, Microsoft certifications, etc.). However, benefits cannot be paid for costs of classes to prepare individuals to take such exams. This stands in stark contrast with tests for admission to an institution of higher learning (e.g., SAT, ACT, GRE, LSAT, etc.) for which VA educational assistance can be paid for preparatory courses and reimbursement of test fees.

DIVEST THE WASHINGTON AQUEDUCT
Corps of Engineers

The Budget proposes to divest the Federal Government of the Washington Aqueduct (Aqueduct), which is the wholesale water supply system for Washington, D.C.; Arlington County, Virginia; the City of Falls Church, Virginia; and parts of Fairfax County, Virginia. Eliminating the Corps' role in local water supply and increasing the State, local, or private sector's role would encourage a more efficient allocation of economic resources and mitigate risk to taxpayers.

Funding Summary
(In millions of dollars)

	2019	2020	2021	2022	2023	2024	2025	2026	2027	2028	2019-23	2019-28
Proposed Change from Current Law............................	0	0	-120	0	0	0	0	0	0	0	-120	-120

Justification

The Army Corps of Engineers (Corps) is a Federal agency that owns and operates the Aqueduct, which is the only local water supply system in the Nation owned and operated by the Corps. The Aqueduct's wholesale customers pay the Corps to cover the cost of routine Aqueduct operations. The Corps borrowed $75 million from the Treasury in the mid-1990s to pay for certain capital improvements (Aqueduct customers are in the process of repaying that amount to the U.S. Treasury). Ownership of local water supply is best carried out by State or local government or the private sector where there are appropriate market and regulatory incentives.

REFORM INLAND WATERWAYS FINANCING
Corps of Engineers

The Administration proposes to reform the laws governing the Inland Waterways Trust Fund, including establishing an annual fee to increase the amount paid by commercial navigation users of the inland waterways. The additional revenue would support infrastructure investment and economic growth by helping finance the users' share of future capital investments, as well as 10 percent of the operation and maintenance cost in these waterways. The current excise tax on diesel fuel used in inland waterways commerce will not produce the revenue needed to cover these costs.

Funding Summary
(In millions of dollars)

	2019	2020	2021	2022	2023	2024	2025	2026	2027	2028	2019-23	2019-28
Proposed Change from Current Law............	-178	-178	-178	-178	-178	-178	-178	-178	-178	-178	-890	-1,780

Justification

The Army Corps of Engineers (Corps) inland waterways program constructs, operates, and maintains 229 lock chambers at 187 dam sites, and other features that make it possible to move cargo by barge on 12,000 miles of developed inland channels. Nearly all of the Federal cost to support navigation on the inland waterways involves Corps spending on the locks and dams—to construct, operate, maintain, repair, replace, and rehabilitate them; and to expand the level of service that they provide. Under current law, barge owners pay 50 percent of the cost of most inland waterways capital investments (with the exception of the Olmsted Locks and Dam Project). The General Fund pays the other 50 percent of these costs, plus all of the operation and maintenance. The central financing challenge now facing the inland waterways program is that the current diesel fuel tax (which the Congress increased from 20 cents per gallon to 29 cents per gallon in 2014) will not generate enough revenue to support the user-financed 50 percent share of the capital investments that will be needed over the next 10 to 15 years. The Budget proposes to increase revenue to support additional work on the inland waterways through a new user fee. This proposal would raise just over $1.7 billion over the 10 year window to finance part of the cost of anticipated capital investment projects and operation and maintenance activities on the inland waterways.

INCREASE EMPLOYEE CONTRIBUTIONS TO 50 PERCENT OF COST, PHASED IN AT ONE PERCENT PER YEAR
Office of Personnel Management

This proposal would increase Federal employee contributions to the Federal Employees Retirement System (FERS) such that the employee and employer would each pay half the normal cost. For Federal workers in certain occupations, such as law enforcement and firefighting, employee contributions would increase, but the Government would continue to pay a higher share of the normal cost.

By increasing the employee share, the Federal Government's costs would be reduced. To mitigate the impact on employees, this provision would be phased in over several years, with individuals contributing an additional one percent of their salary each year.

Funding Summary
(In millions of dollars)

	2019	2020	2021	2022	2023	2024	2025	2026	2027	2028	2019-23	2019-28
Proposed Change from Current Law........................	0	-2,267	-4,602	-6,442	-8,068	-9,441	-9,456	-9,470	-9,480	-9,479	-21,379	-68,705

Note: Savings exclude non-scoreable impacts due to the loss of intragovernmental employer share receipts. Savings also do not include the Budget proposal to reduce the discretionary spending limits to reflect the reductions in normal cost contributions paid by Federal agencies.

Justification

According to an April 25, 2017 Congressional Budget Office (CBO) Report,[1] Federal employees are, on average, compensated with combined pay and benefits 17 percent higher than the private sector. The disparity is overwhelmingly attributable to benefits. As the CBO study shows, in comparison to the private sector, the Federal Government continues to offer a very generous package of retirement benefits, even when controlling for certain characteristics of workers. At large private sector firms, only approximately 35 percent of workers had access to a combination of defined benefit and defined contribution programs.

Another benefit of this proposal is that it would generally equalize the percentage of salary that civilian workers pay toward their pension benefit. At present, newer cohorts of employees pay a higher percentage than do those with greater seniority.

The Administration has lessened the impact of the proposal to increase employee contribution to FERS, by phasing in the implementation with a one percent increase in contributions each year. In the context of the broader labor environment, the Administration believes the implementation and phasing in of retirement benefit changes will not impact the Federal Government's recruiting and retention efforts.

Citations

[1] Congressional Budget Office: *Comparing the Compensation of Federal and Private-Sector Employees, 2011 to 2015,* (April 2017).

[2] Bureau of Labor Statistics: *National Compensation Survey,* (2016).

MODIFY THE GOVERNMENT CONTRIBUTION RATE TO FEDERAL EMPLOYEES HEALTH BENEFITS PROGRAM PREMIUMS

Office of Personnel Management

This proposal would revise the government contribution rate to base it on a plan's score from the Federal Employees Health Benefits (FEHB) Program Plan Performance Assessment. Currently all FEHB carriers participate in the assessment, which includes 19 measures of health outcomes, quality, and efficiency. Under this proposal, the Government contribution would range between 65-75 percent depending on a plan's performance. This proposal would encourage enrollment in high-performing health plans.

Funding Summary
(In millions of dollars)

	2019	2020	2021	2022	2023	2024	2025	2026	2027	2028	2019-23	2019-28
Proposed Change from Current Law..........................	0	0	-192	-301	-321	-342	-363	-387	-412	-439	-814	-2,757

Justification

FEHB covers approximately 8.2 million lives: about 2.1 million active employees; 1.9 million annuitants; and spouses and dependents. The Government contribution to premiums is currently set in statute at 72 percent of the weighted average of all plan premiums, not to exceed 75 percent of any given plan's premium. Under the current structure, enrollees have few incentives to choose less expensive, higher value plans. This proposal would incentivize enrollees to select high-performing, high-value plans by making them more affordable. The proposal would also provide carriers with greater incentive to compete on price and quality, help driving down overall program costs.

REDUCE FEDERAL RETIREMENT BENEFITS
Office of Personnel Management

This proposal would reduce the cost of Federal employee annuities via revisions to the Federal Employees Retirement System (FERS) and the Civil Service Retirement System (CSRS). The proposal would eliminate cost of living adjustments (COLAs) for FERS retirees, and would reduce CSRS retiree COLAs by 0.5 percent. It would also eliminate the FERS Special Retirement Supplement for those employees who retire before Social Security eligibility age, calculate employees' annuity based on the "High-5" salary years instead of "High-3" salary years, and reduce the "G" fund interest rate. The employee compensation landscape continues to evolve. Private sector employers provide a smaller share of compensation in the form of retirement benefits than does the Federal Government. Recent decades have seen a dramatic shift by private employers away from defined benefit retirement programs. The Federal Government, in contrast, provides a much greater share of its employees' compensation in the form of retirement benefits—including pension benefits and post-retirement health care benefits. The provisions of this proposal would bring Federal retirement benefits more in line with the private sector, while reducing their long-term costs.

Funding Summary
(In millions of dollars)

	2019	2020	2021	2022	2023	2024	2025	2026	2027	2028	2019-23	2019-28
Eliminate FERS COLA, Reduce CSRS COLA by 0.5%.................	-1,119	-1,783	-2,524	-3,350	-4,247	-5,213	-6,250	-7,357	-8,539	-9,798	-13,023	-50,180
Eliminate Special Retirement Supplement.........................	-497	-867	-1,274	-1,596	-1,818	-2,028	-2,290	-2,540	-2,762	-3,003	-6,052	-18,675
Change Retirement Calculation from High-3 years to High-5 years....................	-277	-339	-405	-476	-549	-623	-698	-778	-860	-944	-2,046	-5,949
Reduce the G Fund Interest Rate................................	-694	-382	-1,142	-671	-798	-877	-957	-1,052	-1,132	-1,216	-3,687	-8,921
Total..................	-2,587	-3,371	-5,345	-6,093	-7,412	-8,741	-10,195	-11,727	-13,293	-14,961	-24,808	-83,725

Note: Savings exclude non-scoreable impacts due to the loss of intragovernmental employer share receipts. Savings also do not include the Budget proposal to reduce the discretionary spending limits to reflect the reductions in normal cost contributions paid by Federal agencies.

Justification

According to an April 25, 2017 Congressional Budget Office (CBO) Report,[1] Federal employees are, on average, compensated with combined pay and benefits 17 percent higher than the private sector. The disparity is overwhelmingly attributable to benefits. As the CBO study shows, in comparison to the private sector, the Federal Government continues to offer a very generous package of retirement benefits, even when controlling for certain characteristics of workers. At large private sector firms, only approximately 35 percent of workers had access to a combination of defined benefit and defined contribution programs.[2]

Eliminate FERS COLA, Reduce CSRS COLA by 0.5 percent—FERS and CSRS COLAs for annuitants are currently determined based on statutory formulas tied to the Consumer Price Index. However, FERS annuitants are somewhat protected from economic effects, because their retirement packages include Social Security benefits and TSP, in addition to the FERS annuity. Eliminating the FERS COLA and reducing the CSRS COLA payments would reduce both FERS and CSRS annuity benefits, bringing compensation more in line with the private sector.

Eliminate the Special Retirement Supplement—When a FERS employee retires before Social Security eligibility age, and meets certain employment longevity requirements, they currently receive a supplement in addition to the FERS annuity and TSP payouts. This supplement partially replaces the Social Security portion of the retirement package. When private sector employees retire before Social Security eligibility age, no such supplement is provided. This proposal would eliminate this "extra" benefit, which is not typically provided in private sector annuity plans.

Change Retirement Calculation from High-3 years to High-5 years—Currently, Federal retirement annuity calculations are based on the average of the Federal employee's three highest salary-earning years. Private sector pension companies commonly base employee annuity calculations on the employee's five highest salary-earning years, a formula more representative of an employee's career earnings track record. Switching the Federal employee annuity formula from a "High-3" to a "High-5" calculation would create greater alignment with the private sector.

Reduce the G Fund Interest Rate—This proposal includes a change to the "G" fund, an investment vehicle available only through the Thrift Savings Plan (TSP), a defined contribution plan for Federal Government employees. G Fund investors currently benefit from receiving a medium-term rate of return on what is essentially a short-term security. Basing the yield on a short-term T-bill rate instead of the current rate (an average of medium and long term Treasury bond rates) would reduce both the projected rate of return to investors and the cost of the fund to the Treasury.

Citations

[1] Congressional Budget Office: *Comparing the Compensation of Federal and Private-Sector Employees, 2011 to 2015,* (April 2017).

[2] Bureau of Labor Statistics: *National Compensation Survey,* (2016).

DIVEST TENNESSEE VALLEY AUTHORITY TRANSMISSION ASSETS
Other Independent Agencies

The Budget proposes to sell the transmission assets of the Tennessee Valley Authority (TVA). The private sector is best suited to own and operate electricity transmission assets. Eliminating the Federal Government's role in owning and operating transmission assets encourages a more efficient allocation of economic resources and mitigates unnecessary risk to taxpayers.

Funding Summary
(In millions of dollars)

	2019	2020	2021	2022	2023	2024	2025	2026	2027	2028	2019-23	2019-28
Proposed Change from Current Law............................	241	-3,760	-19	-19	-19	-19	-19	-19	-19	-19	-3,576	-3,671

Justification

The Budget proposes to sell the electricity transmission assets of the Tennessee Valley Authority. The vast majority of the Nation's electricity infrastructure is owned and operated by for-profit investor owned utilities. Ownership of transmission assets is best carried out by the private sector where there are appropriate market and regulatory incentives.

ELIMINATE THE SECURITIES AND EXCHANGE COMMISSION'S RESERVE FUND
Other Independent Agencies

The Budget proposes to restore the Securities and Exchange Commission's (SEC) accountability to the American taxpayer by eliminating its reserve fund, created by the Dodd-Frank Wall Street Reform and Consumer Protection Act (Dodd-Frank Act).

Funding Summary
(In millions of dollars)

	2019	2020	2021	2022	2023	2024	2025	2026	2027	2028	2019-23	2019-28
Proposed Change from Current Law............................	0	-17	-41	-50	-50	-50	-50	-50	-50	-50	-158	-408

Justification

Created by the Dodd-Frank Act, the SEC's mandatory reserve fund has come to represent an extension of the Agency's regular appropriation rather than the emergency reserve it was intended to be. This proposal would restore the SEC's accountability by diverting reserve fund resources to the General Fund for deficit reduction and requiring the SEC to request any additional appropriations from the Congress beginning in 2020.

ENACT SPECTRUM LICENSE USER FEE
Other Independent Agencies

The Budget proposes to provide the Federal Communications Commission (FCC) with new authority to use economic mechanisms, such as fees, as a spectrum management tool.

Funding Summary
(In millions of dollars)

	2019	2020	2021	2022	2023	2024	2025	2026	2027	2028	2019-23	2019-28
Proposed Change from Current Law.............	-50	-150	-300	-450	-500	-500	-500	-500	-500	-500	-1,450	-3,950

Justification

To promote the efficient use of the electromagnetic spectrum, the Administration proposes to provide FCC with new authority to use economic mechanisms, such as fees, as a spectrum management tool. The FCC would be authorized to set user fees on unauctioned spectrum licenses based on spectrum-management principles. Fees would be phased in over time as part of an ongoing rulemaking process to determine the appropriate application and level of fees that maximize spectrum utilization.

REFORM THE POSTAL SERVICE
Other Independent Agencies

The Budget proposes to reform the United States Postal Service (USPS) to allow the Agency to meet its financial and service obligations with business revenue, as intended, rather than a taxpayer-financed bailout. The reform proposal includes changes to USPS's rate setting; delivery schedule and methods; and updated health and pension costs consistent with Government-wide reforms proposed for Federal employees.

Funding Summary
(In millions of dollars)

	2019	2020	2021	2022	2023	2024	2025	2026	2027	2028	2019-23	2019-28
Postal Reform (Postal Service Effects, Off-Budget, No PAYGO)...............................	-1,027	-1,141	-1,220	-721	-490	-388	0	0	0	0	-4,599	-4,987
Postal Reform (OPM Effects, On-Budget, PAYGO)..............	-3,565	-3,445	-3,310	-3,780	-3,963	-4,050	-4,436	-4,392	-4,308	-4,254	-18,063	-39,503
Total.......................................	-4,592	-4,586	-4,530	-4,501	-4,453	-4,438	-4,436	-4,392	-4,308	-4,254	-22,662	-44,490

Justification

The USPS business model relies on stable First-Class Mail revenue to support the substantial fixed costs of providing universal mail service to more than 150 million delivery points. However, persistent declines in mail volume resulting from the transition to digital communication have fundamentally undermined this model and USPS has reported multi-billion dollar losses each year since 2007. Since 2012, USPS has prioritized payments to employees and vendors, while defaulting on required payments of more than $5 billion each year to the Office of Personnel Management (OPM) for current and former employee benefits costs. To reverse this trend USPS must be given the ability to address their expenses—including the cost of personnel—and take appropriate actions to balance service levels with revenue.[1] USPS must also have the flexibility to raise the revenue necessary to support their operations.[2]

The Budget proposes a combination of operational reforms and retiree health and pension changes to restore solvency to USPS and ensure that it funds existing commitments to current and former employees from business revenues rather than taxpayer funds. Operational reforms include changes to how rates are set, modification of USPS's delivery schedule, and use of more efficient delivery methods. In addition to Government-wide changes to health and pension programs (see the OPM section of this volume) that will reduce USPS operating costs, the Budget proposes specific Postal reforms to modify USPS's contributions for life and health insurance for employees to be more consistent with Government-wide standards.

In total, the Budget estimates that these reforms would reduce the unified budget deficit by $44 billion over 10 years and result in on-budget savings as the Postal Service resumes statutory payments to on-budget OPM accounts.

Citations

[1] Government Accountability Office: *U.S. Postal Service: Key Considerations for Restoring Fiscal Sustainability*, GAO-17-404T, (February 2017).

[2] United States Postal Service Office of the Inspector General: *Funding the Universal Service Obligation*, RARC-WP-16-005, (March 2016).

RESTRUCTURE THE CONSUMER FINANCIAL PROTECTION BUREAU
Other Independent Agencies

The Budget proposes to restructure the Consumer Financial Protection Bureau (CFPB), limit the Agency's mandatory funding in 2019, and provide discretionary appropriations to fund the Agency beginning in 2020.

Funding Summary
(In millions of dollars)

	2019	2020	2021	2022	2023	2024	2025	2026	2027	2028	2019-23	2019-28
Proposed Change from Current Law............................	-147	-610	-656	-672	-687	-704	-720	-737	-755	-773	-2,772	-6,461

Note: Savings reflect reductions to estimated mandatory funding under current law. Appropriations in 2020 – 2029 and beyond would be provided under the discretionary caps.

Justification

CFPB, created by the Dodd-Frank Wall Street Reform and Consumer Protection Act (Dodd-Frank), is an independent agency with a single unaccountable director who is able to draw funding from the Federal Reserve without oversight from the Congress. The Agency also has broad authority to unilaterally develop and enforce regulations irrespective of congressional intent or economic impact.

The CFPB's short history is rife with examples of the poor financial and personnel management decisions that can result from this form of unchecked authority. For example, the Government Accountability Office (GAO) found multiple issues with CFPB's design and implementation of its internal controls over financial reporting.[1] The Agency also faced personnel management challenges that resulted in congressional and GAO investigations regarding allegations of discrimination and retaliation against employees.[2] The Budget proposes to address these issues through legislative reforms to restructure the Agency, bring accountability to its leadership, and safeguard against potential abuses of these powers.

The proposed reforms would impose financial discipline, reduce wasteful spending, and ensure appropriate congressional oversight, by subjecting the Agency to discretionary appropriations starting in 2020. The proposal would also cap transfers by the Federal Reserve Board to CFPB during 2019 to $485 million, equivalent to the 2015 level. To prevent actions that unduly burden the financial industry and limit consumer choice, the proposal restricts CFPB's broad enforcement authority over Federal consumer law. These changes would allow CFPB to focus its efforts on enforcing enacted consumer protection laws and eliminate the functions that allowed the Agency to become an unaccountable bureaucracy with unchecked regulatory authority. To allow for an efficient transition, the Budget proposes a two-year restructuring period with reforms fully effectuated by 2021.

Citations

[1] Government Accountability Office: *Improvements Needed in CFPB's Internal Controls and Accounting Procedures*, GAO-16-5222R, (June 2016); Government Accountability Office: *Selected Agencies' Activities Supported by Contracts and Public Affairs Staff*, GAO-17-711, (September 2017).

[2] Government Accountability Office: *Additional Actions Needed to Support a Fair and Inclusive Workplace*, GAO-16-61, (May 2016).

www.ingramcontent.com/pod-product-compliance
Lightning Source LLC
Chambersburg PA
CBHW080238270326
41926CB00020B/4291